# AIR-FRYER
## COOKBOOK

# AIR-FRYER
## COOKBOOK

### Quick, healthy and delicious recipes for beginners

101 tried-and-tested recipes

**JENNY TSCHIESCHE**

PHOTOGRAPHY BY CLARE WINFIELD

RYLAND PETERS & SMALL
LONDON • NEW YORK

**Dedication**

*For my husband Werner and children, Amalie and Sam,*
*without whose taste buds this book would not have been possible.*

**Art director**  Leslie Harrington
**Editor**  Gillian Haslam
**Production manager**  Gordana
  Simakovic
**Editorial director**  Julia Charles
**Publisher**  Cindy Richards

**Food stylist**  Maud Eden
**Prop stylist**  Max Robinson
**Indexer**  Hilary Bird

First published in 2022 by
Ryland Peters & Small
20–21 Jockey's Fields
London WC1R 4BW
and 341 E 116th St
New York NY 10029
www.rylandpeters.com

11

Text copyright © Jenny Tschiesche
2022
Design and photographs copyright
© Ryland Peters & Small 2022

ISBN: 978-1-78879-424-4

Printed in China

A CIP record for this book is available
from the British Library. US Library of
Congress Cataloging-in-Publication
Data has been applied for.

**Notes:**
• Both British (Metric) and American
(Imperial plus US cups) are included
in these recipes for your convenience,
however it is important to work with
one set of measurements and not
alternate between the two within
a recipe.
• All spoon measurements are level
unless otherwise specified.
• All eggs are medium (UK) or large
(US), unless specified as large, in
which case US extra-large should be
used. Uncooked or partially cooked
eggs should not be served to the very
old, frail, young children, pregnant
women or those with compromised
immune systems.
• The air-fryer should be preheated
to the specified temperatures.
• Whenever butter is called for within
these recipes, unsalted butter should
be used unless otherwise specified.
• When a recipe calls for the grated
zest of citrus fruit, buy unwaxed fruit
and wash well before using. If you can
only find treated fruit, scrub well in
warm soapy water before using.

MIX
Paper | Supporting
responsible forestry
FSC® C008047
FSC
www.fsc.org

# CONTENTS

Introduction 6

Basic Recipes 9

Fries & Snacks 18

Meat 40

Poultry 58

Fish & Seafood 74

Vegetarian & Vegan 88

Side Dishes 110

Sweet Things 126

Index 142

Acknowledgements 144

# INTRODUCTION

Many millions of people all over the world have already discovered that air-fryers can produce delicious food – you may have heard friends rave about the crispy, crunchy fries made using their air-fryers, without any need to use a deep fat fryer or the copious amounts of oil it demands. Once you've tried this low-fat way of cooking fries, you won't go back. However, if you think an air-fryer is only for fries, you are about to have your mind blown.

If you're just getting to grips with this latest cooking revolution, then it's best to think of an air-fryer as not only a healthier alternative to a deep fat fryer, but also as a mini oven. Heat radiates from a heating element and a powerful fan circulates the hot air around (as in convection cooking). The air-fryer is much more efficient than your main oven, too. Think of how many times you heat your entire oven only to cook a small amount of food, wasting all that energy. Now compare that to heating up your mini oven (i.e. your air-fryer) in just 1–2 minutes and cooking your food in super-fast time, too. The speed factor associated with air-frying is due to the convection mechanism used for preheating and maintaining constant heat. This means that alongside the microwave, the air-fryer is the most efficient mechanism for heating food. However, the microwave is never going to give food that tasty crispiness, crunchiness and caramelisation that the air-fryer can produce.

Whether you're looking for healthier alternatives to fries, a quick and tasty way to cook falafel, fish or meat, crispy and crunchy homemade chicken nuggets, arancini or fish fingers/sticks, or tasty snacks like trail mix or granola, the air-fryer allows you the opportunity to make these dishes your way, quickly.

As you flick through this book you'll see the words 'fried', 'roasted' or 'baked' in some recipe titles. I've simply used these words to give you an idea of what to expect from the finished dish, as technically speaking all recipes are air-fried.

This book is designed to help you enjoy air-frying and to explore all the cooking possibilities the air-fryer can offer. Once you've mastered the recipes in this book, don't be afraid to experiment with new ingredients. I'd love to hear from you on Instagram (@lunchboxdoctor) with photos of recipes you have enjoyed from this book and any new dishes that you've been inspired to create.

## SUGGESTED ADDITIONAL EQUIPMENT

There are a few additional pieces of kitchen equipment that will allow you to use the air-fryer for the greatest range of recipes. These items are:

- Meat thermometer
- Air-fryer liners, although you can easily use a piece of pierced parchment paper instead (the pierced holes allow the hot air to circulate)
- A 15 x 15-cm/6 x 6-in. baking pan
- A gratin dish that fits inside your air-fryer and is suitable for high heat
- A spray bottle for oil

These can all be easily purchased online or from a good kitchenware shop.

## TIPS FOR USING YOUR AIR-FRYER

Air-frying, although low in fat, is not completely without fat and for this reason I recommend buying a spray bottle in which you keep olive oil or avocado oil (keep this spray bottle in a dark place to stop the oil within it becoming damaged by light exposure).

Spritz the foods before they go into the air-fryer, especially breaded foods as this is how you're going to achieve that delicious, golden crumb.

Throughout the book I have specified standard temperatures for recipes, but some air-fryers have some quirky temperature settings. Just use the closest setting to that specified in the recipe that your air-fryer has. For example, if I specify 200°C/400°F and your air-fryer has 199°C/390°F, then use that.

Use your meat thermometer to work out when food is cooked enough. This tends to relate to meat, fish and poultry, but also to the arancini on page 102.

Space food out in your air-fryer to allow even baking. Air has to flow around the food in order for it to become crunchy and/or caramelised.

Many of the recipes in this book benefit from a shake of the air-fryer's drawer partway through cooking – this is always stated in the method. Some recipes are too delicate or simply don't need a shake, so only shake the drawer if instructed.

Remember to clean your air-fryer after every use, but do allow it to cool before doing so. This way you are less likely to cause damage to the lining of the air-fryer drawer.

Don't forget that the air-fryer is not only to be used for cooking new dishes. It can be used to reheat things you've already made or items of food from your freezer. It's invaluable as a reheating tool in a family kitchen.

## DRIED BREADCRUMBS

**100 g/3¹/₂ oz. sourdough or gluten-free fresh breadcrumbs (1–2 slices bread whizzed in a food processor)**

Save money by making your own breadcrumbs rather than buying readymade ones. This is a great way to use up bread that has reached its use-by date.

Preheat the air-fryer to 180°C/350°F.

Spread the fresh breadcrumbs out on a baking sheet that fits inside your air-fryer. Place in the preheated air-fryer and air-fry for 2 minutes, then remove and allow to cool before storing in an airtight container.

## SOURDOUGH CROUTONS

**3 thick slices sourdough bread**
**3 tablespoons olive oil**
**¹/₈ teaspoon salt**

**SERVES 2**

These chunky croutons are so crispy and flavoursome. They're a great way to use up slightly older sourdough which, let's face it, doesn't (and shouldn't) last long. Perfect for topping salads and soups or in panzanella – a simple yet tasty Tuscan dish of croutons, tomatoes and olive oil.

Preheat the air-fryer to 200°C/400°F.

Chop the bread into 2.5-cm/1-in. cubes. Mix these in a bowl with the oil and salt.

Add the bread cubes to the preheated air-fryer in a single layer and air-fry for 4 minutes, shaking the air-fryer drawer to toss halfway through cooking.

Serve the croutons whilst crispy and crunchy.

# SOFT-BOILED EGGS

**4 eggs**

**SERVES 2**

This is a brilliantly quick and easy way to prepare soft-boiled/cooked eggs, and there's no need to wash the air-fryer after cooking. These are great served with roasted asparagus spears (see page 116).

Preheat the air-fryer to 180°C/350°F.

Add the eggs to the preheated air-fryer and air-fry for 6 minutes. Remove and leave to stand for 1 minute, then knock the tops off the eggs and serve.

# TOAST

**1–2 slices bread (gluten-free if you wish)**

**SERVES 1**

A simple but useful tip for anything from this book that you'd like to eat either with or on toast.

Preheat the air-fryer to 180°C/350°F.

Add the bread to the preheated air-fryer and air-fry for 1 minute, then turn over and cook the other side for a further minute.

# FRENCH TOAST

1 large egg
80 ml/5 tablespoons milk
 (dairy-free if you wish)
½ teaspoon vanilla extract
¼ teaspoon ground cinnamon
2 slices sourdough bread
maple syrup and crispy bacon
 (see below), to serve

**SERVES 1–2**

Air-frying is a healthier way to enjoy this popular breakfast. Delicious served with bacon and maple syrup, or you opt for some fresh berries and yogurt.

Beat the egg in a shallow bowl, then whisk in the milk, vanilla extract and cinnamon until well combined and frothy in appearance. Dip both sides of each slice of sourdough bread into the mixture. Give the bread a chance to soak up the mixture before removing.

Preheat the air-fryer to 200°C/400°F.

Add the slices of bread to the preheated air-fryer and air-fry for 3 minutes on one side, then turn over and cook for a further 2 minutes.

Serve with maple syrup and crispy bacon.

# CRISPY BACON & CRISPY LARDONS

6 slices bacon or
 125 g/4½ oz. lardons

**SERVES 2–3**

Ideal for serving on avocado toast, with French toast or to top salads.

Preheat the air-fryer to 180°C/350°F.

To cook the bacon, place in the preheated air-fryer. Air-fry for 3 minutes, then turn over and cook for a further 3 minutes, then serve.

To cook the lardons, place in the preheated air-fryer. Air-fry for 2 minutes, then turn over and cook for a further 2 minutes, then serve.

# CRISPY CHICKPEAS

400-g/14-oz. can chickpeas, drained and rinsed
1 tablespoon olive oil
1 teaspoon unrefined sugar
½ teaspoon smoked paprika
¼ teaspoon cayenne pepper
1 teaspoon salt

**SERVES 4 AS A SALAD TOPPER OR SNACK**

Ideal as a snack on their own, as a salad topper or serve in a wrap with some hummus and salad.

Preheat the air-fryer to 200°C/400°F.

Toss the chickpeas in the oil, sugar, spices and seasoning, ensuring they are evenly coated. Add the chickpeas to the preheated air-fryer and air-fry for 8–10 minutes, shaking the drawer a couple of times during cooking.

# HALLOUMI CROUTONS

225 g/8 oz. halloumi, roughly chopped into 2-cm/¾-in. cubes
1½ teaspoons olive oil

**SERVES 4 AS CROUTONS FOR A SALAD**

Perfect for topping a summer salad.

Preheat the air-fryer to 200°C/400°F.

Toss the halloumi cubes in the olive oil. Add the halloumi to the preheated air-fryer and air-fry for 5 minutes, shaking the drawer once during cooking.

# CARAMELISED WALNUTS & PECANS

100 g/3½ oz. mixed walnuts and
   pecans
1 egg white
1 tablespoon melted and cooled
   butter (do not use unsalted
   butter)
2 teaspoons unrefined or coconut
   sugar
½ teaspoon ground cinnamon

**SERVES 4**

These nuts are not too sweet but just caramelly
enough to really elevate the flavour and texture
of a savoury salad or soup.

Preheat the air-fryer to 150°C/300°F.

Mix the egg white, melted butter, sugar and cinnamon
in a bowl. Toss in the nuts and stir until coated. Spread
the nuts out on an air-fryer liner or a piece of pierced
baking parchment and add the paper and nuts to the
preheated air-fryer.

Air-fry for 4 minutes, then turn the nuts over and cook
for a further 2 minutes. Remove from the air-fryer and
leave to cool thoroughly. These will keep in a jar for up
to a week.

# MAPLE TRAIL MIX

75 g/½ cup almonds
50 g/½ cup pecan halves
20 g/¼ cup sultanas/golden
   raisins
20 g/½ cup coconut flakes/chips
1 tablespoon melted coconut oil
1 tablespoon maple syrup
⅛ teaspoon salt
½ teaspoon vanilla extract

**SERVES 4**

A delicious, nutritious on-the-go snack that you
can make in minutes.

Preheat the air-fryer to 180°C/350°F.

Mix all ingredients in a bowl. Add the mix to the
preheated air-fryer, preferably on an air-fryer liner or a
piece of pierced parchment paper so that smaller pieces
do not fall into the drawer below. Air-fry for 6 minutes,
shaking the drawer once during cooking.

Allow to cool, then then enjoy.

# FRIES & SNACKS

# POTATO FRIES

2 large potatoes (baking
    potato size)
1 teaspoon olive oil
salt

**SERVES 2**

One of the reasons that air-fryers have such a good reputation is due to their ability to produce chips with far less fat. That said, you still want those healthier chips to have great flavour and that's what this recipe delivers.

Peel the potatoes and slice into fries about 1.5 x 1.5cm/¾ x ¾ in. by the length of the potato. Submerge the fries in a bowl of cold water and place in the fridge for about 10 minutes.

Meanwhile, preheat the air-fryer to 160°C/325°F.

Drain the fries thoroughly, then toss in the oil and season. Tip into the preheated air-fryer in a single layer (you may need to cook them in two batches, depending on the size of your air-fryer). Air-fry for 15 minutes, tossing once during cooking by shaking the air-fryer drawer, then increase the temperature of the air-fryer to 200°C/400°F and cook for a further 3 minutes. Serve immediately.

# SWEET POTATO FRIES

2 medium sweet potatoes
2 teaspoons olive oil
½ teaspoon salt
½ teaspoon chilli/hot red
    pepper flakes
½ teaspoon smoked paprika

**SERVES 4**

Fries made from sweet potatoes rather than regular potatoes have gained great popularity with those who like sweeter fries. They taste great with mayo, and even better with garlic mayo!

Preheat the air-fryer to 190°C/375°F.

Peel the sweet potatoes and slice into fries about 1 x 1 cm/ ½ x ½ in. by the length of the potato. Toss the sweet potato fries in the oil, salt, chilli and paprika, making sure every fry is coated.

Tip into the preheated air-fryer in a single layer (you may need to cook them in two batches, depending on the size of your air-fryer). Air-fry for 10 minutes, turning once halfway during cooking. Serve immediately.

# SWEDE FRIES

1 medium swede/rutabaga
½ teaspoon salt
½ teaspoon freshly ground
   black pepper
1½ teaspoons dried thyme
1 tablespoon olive oil

**SERVES 4**

Ideal for those who love the idea of fries but want a lower carb alternative.

Preheat the air-fryer to 160°C/325°F.

Peel the swede/rutabaga and slice into fries about 6 x 1 cm/2½ x ½ in., then toss the fries in the salt, pepper, thyme and oil, making sure every fry is coated.

Tip into the preheated air-fryer in a single layer (you may need to cook them in two batches, depending on the size of your air-fryer) and air-fry for 15 minutes, shaking the drawer halfway through. Then increase the temperature to 180°C/350°F and cook for a further 5 minutes. Serve immediately.

# PLANTAIN FRIES

1 ripe plantain (yellow and brown
   outside skin)
1 teaspoon olive oil
¼ teaspoon salt

**SERVES 2**

Think of a plantain as a more savoury and starchier version of a banana. Great with a sprinkling of salt.

Preheat the air-fryer to 180°C/350°F.

Peel the plantain and slice into fries about 6 x 1 cm/ 2½ x ½ in. Toss the fries in oil and salt, making sure every fry is coated.

Tip into the preheated air-fryer in a single layer (you may need to cook them in two batches, depending on the size of your air-fryer) and air-fry for 13–14 minutes until brown on the outside and soft on the inside. Serve immediately.

# POLENTA FRIES

800 ml/scant 3½ cups water
1½ vegetable stock cubes
¾ teaspoon dried oregano
¾ teaspoon freshly ground
  black pepper
200 g/1⅓ cups quick-cook
  polenta/cornmeal
2 teaspoons olive oil
55 g/6 tablespoons plain/
  all-purpose flour (gluten-free
  if you wish)
garlic mayonnaise, to serve

**SERVES 6**

A cornmeal-based alternative to potato fries. Of Italian origin, these make an ideal side dish to Aubergine Parmigiana (see page 94) or are great served as a snack.

Bring the water and stock cubes to the boil in a saucepan with the oregano and black pepper. Stir in the polenta/cornmeal and continue to stir until the mixture becomes significantly more solid and is hard to stir – this should take about 5–6 minutes.

Grease a 15 x 15-cm/6 x 6-in. baking pan with some of the olive oil. Tip the polenta into the baking pan, smoothing down with the back of a wet spoon. Leave to cool at room temperature for about 30 minutes, then pop into the fridge for at least an hour.

Remove the polenta from the fridge and carefully tip out onto a chopping board. Slice the polenta into fingers 7.5 x 1 x 2 cm/3 x ½ x ¾ in. Roll the polenta fingers in the flour, then spray or drizzle the remaining olive oil over the fingers.

Preheat the air-fryer to 200°C/400°F.

Lay the fingers apart from one another in a single layer in the preheated air-fryer (you may need to cook these in batches, depending on the size of your air-fryer). Air-fry for 9 minutes, turning once halfway through cooking. Serve immediately with garlic mayonnaise.

# COURGETTE FRIES

1 courgette/zucchini
3 tablespoons plain/all-purpose flour (gluten-free if you wish)
¼ teaspoon salt
¼ teaspoon freshly ground black pepper
60 g/¾ cup dried breadcrumbs (gluten-free if you wish; see page 9)
1 teaspoon dried oregano
20 g/¼ cup finely grated Parmesan
1 egg, beaten

SERVES 2

If my children are anything to go by, then courgettes/zucchini are not a favourite vegetable. However, try coating them in this seasoned cheesy crumb as they seem to think it is rather delicious!

Preheat the air-fryer to 180°C/350°F.

Slice the courgette/zucchini into fries about 1.5 x 1.5 x 5 cm/⅝ x ⅝ x 2 in.

Season the flour with salt and pepper. Combine the breadcrumbs with the oregano and Parmesan.

Dip the courgettes/zucchini in the flour (shaking off any excess flour), then the egg, then the seasoned breadcrumbs.

Add the fries to the preheated air-fryer and air-fry for 15 minutes. They should be crispy on the outside but soft on the inside. Serve immediately.

# AVOCADO FRIES

35 g/¼ cup plain/all-purpose flour (gluten free if you wish)
½ teaspoon chilli/chili powder
1 egg, beaten
50 g/heaped ½ cup dried breadcrumbs (gluten-free if you wish; see page 9)
1 avocado, skin and stone removed, and each half sliced lengthways
salt and freshly ground black pepper

SERVES 2

Crispy on the outside and creamy on the inside, these avocado fries are a delight. They make a great side dish, but are even better served as a snack with some tomato salsa alongside.

Preheat the air-fryer to 200°C/400°F.

In a bowl combine the flour and chilli/chili powder, then season with salt and pepper. Place the beaten egg in a second bowl and the breadcrumbs in a third bowl.

Dip each avocado slice in the seasoned flour (shaking off any excess), then the egg and finally the breadcrumbs.

Add the breaded avocado slices to the preheated air-fryer and air-fry for 6 minutes, turning after 4 minutes. Serve immediately.

# CUMIN SHOESTRING CARROTS

300 g/10½ oz. carrots
1 teaspoon cornflour/cornstarch
1 teaspoon ground cumin
¼ teaspoon salt
1 tablespoon olive oil
garlic mayonnaise, to serve

**SERVES 2**

Sweet and spicy, carrots and cumin combine so well. Serve as a snack or as a side dish.

Preheat the air-fryer to 200°C/400°F.

Peel the carrots and cut into thin fries, roughly 10 cm x 1 cm x 5 mm/4 x ½ x ¼ in. Toss the carrots in a bowl with all the other ingredients.

Add the carrots to the preheated air-fryer and air-fry for 9 minutes, shaking the drawer of the air-fryer a couple of times during cooking. Serve with garlic mayo on the side.

# WHOLE MINI PEPPERS

9 whole mini (bell) peppers
1 teaspoon olive oil
¼ teaspoon salt

**SERVES 2**

These make a great snack or a side dish to any of the breaded recipes in this book. The air-fryer brings out the natural sweetness of these mini peppers, they add colour to the plate and they are simply melt-in-the-mouth delicious.

Preheat the air-fryer to 180°C/350°F.

Place the peppers in a baking dish that fits in for your air-fryer and drizzle over the oil, then sprinkle over the salt.

Add the dish to the preheated air-fryer and air-fry for 10–12 minutes, depending on how 'chargrilled' you like your peppers.

# SPRING ROLLS

4 rice paper wrappers
2 tablespoons freshly chopped
  coriander/cilantro
1 yellow (bell) pepper, thinly sliced
  lengthways
2 carrots, very thinly sliced
  lengthways
200 g/7 oz. cooked chicken
  (ideal for leftovers from
  Whole Chicken, see page 72),
  shredded
1 teaspoon avocado oil or olive oil
Lime-Almond Satay Sauce (see
  page 87), to serve

**MAKES 4**

The crispiness created when air-frying these rice paper
wrappers contrasts well with the moist chicken and
vegetable-based filling. The satay dipping sauce brings all
these flavours and textures together wonderfully well.

Dip a rice paper wrapper into warm water, then remove and
allow the excess water to drip off. Place the wrapper on a clean
chopping board and place the coriander/cilantro first, then the
(bell) pepper, carrot and chicken in a row down the middle. Fold
the bottom of the wrapper up and over the filling, then fold in
the sides, then fold down the top to enclose the filling. Repeat
to make another 3 spring rolls. Brush a little oil over the surface
of each spring roll.

Preheat the air-fryer to 180°C/350°F.

Add the rolls to the preheated air-fryer on an air-fryer
liner or piece of pierced parchment paper. Air-fry for
10 minutes. Serve immediately with the satay
dipping sauce.

# BOCCONCINI BALLS

70 g/½ cup plus ½ tablespoon
 plain/all-purpose flour
 (gluten-free if you wish)
1 egg, beaten
70 g/1 cup dried breadcrumbs
 (gluten-free if you wish; see
 page 9)
10 bocconcini

**SERVES 2**

Bocconcini are small mozzarella balls. In this recipe they're breaded, then cooked in the air-fryer until melted on the inside and crisp and golden on the outside. Think mozzarella sticks but round! These are great served as a snack or with a salad as a light meal.

Preheat the air-fryer to 200°C/400°F.
 Place the flour, egg and breadcrumbs on 3 separate plates. Dip each bocconcini ball first in the flour to coat, then the egg, shaking off any excess before rolling in the breadcrumbs.
 Add the breaded bocconcini to the preheated air-fryer and air-fry for 5 minutes (no need to turn them during cooking). Serve immediately.

# HALLOUMI FRIES

225 g/8 oz. halloumi
40 g/heaped ¼ cup plain/
 all-purpose flour (gluten-free
 if you wish)
½ teaspoon sweet smoked
 paprika
½ teaspoon dried oregano
¼ teaspoon mild chilli/chili
 powder
olive oil or avocado oil, for
 spraying

**SERVES 2**

Golden, crispy and packed full of the flavour you'd expect from this now widely available Cypriot cheese. You may have eaten these in restaurants, but it is so easy to make your own halloumi fries at home using an air-fryer.

Preheat the air-fryer to 180°C/350°F.
 Slice the halloumi into fries roughly 2 x 1.5 cm/¾ x ⅝ in.
 Mix the flour and seasoning in a bowl and dip each halloumi stick into the flour to coat. Spray with a little oil.
 Add the fries to the preheated air-fryer and air-fry for 5 minutes. Serve immediately.

# BABA GANOUSH

1 large aubergine/eggplant, sliced
   in half lengthways
½ teaspoon salt
5 tablespoons olive oil
1 bulb garlic
30 g/2 tablespoons tahini or
   nut butter
2 tablespoons freshly squeezed
   lemon juice
½ teaspoon ground cumin
¼ teaspoon smoked paprika
salt and freshly ground black
   pepper
3 tablespoons freshly chopped
   flat-leaf parsley

**SERVES 4**

This deliciously smoky aubergine/eggplant dip is best
served with pitta chips (see page 39) or crudités.

Preheat the air-fryer to 200°C/400°F.

Lay the aubergine/eggplant halves cut side up. Sprinkle over
the salt, then drizzle over 1 tablespoon of oil. Cut the top off the
garlic bulb, brush the exposed cloves with a little olive oil, then
wrap in foil. Place the aubergine/eggplant and foil-wrapped
garlic in the preheated air-fryer and air-fry for 15–20 minutes
until the inside of the aubergine is soft and buttery in texture.

Scoop the flesh of the aubergine into a bowl. Squeeze out
about 1 tablespoon of the cooked garlic and add to the bowl
with the remaining 4 tablespoons of olive oil, the tahini/nut
butter, lemon juice, spices and salt and pepper to taste. Mix well
and serve with fresh flat-leaf parsley sprinkled over.

# MUHAMMARA

4 romano peppers
4 tablespoons olive oil
100 g/1 cup walnuts
90 g/1 heaped cup dried
   breadcrumbs (see page 9)
1 teaspoon cumin
2 tablespoons pomegranate
   molasses
freshly squeezed juice of
   ½ a lemon
½ teaspoon chilli/chili salt (or salt
   and some chilli/hot red pepper
   flakes combined)
fresh pomegranate seeds,
   to serve

**SERVES 4**

Jam-packed full of flavour, this red pepper and walnut
dip of Syrian origin is a real appetite pleaser. Serve
with crudités or pitta chips (see page 39).

Preheat the air-fryer to 180°C/350°F.

Rub the peppers with ½ teaspoon of the olive oil. Add the
peppers to the preheated air-fryer and air-fry for 8 minutes.

Meanwhile, lightly toast the walnuts by tossing them in
a shallow pan over a medium heat for 3–5 minutes. Allow to
cool, then grind the walnuts in a food processor. Once the
peppers are cooked, chop off the tops and discard most of the
seeds. Add to the food processor with all other ingredients.
Process until smooth. Allow to cool in the fridge, then serve
the dip with pomegranate seeds on top.

# SCOTCH EGGS

3 boiled/cooked eggs (see page 10; if you want them soft-boiled/cooked and runnier in the centre, cook for just 6–7 minutes, or 10 minutes for hard-boiled/cooked)

350 g/12 oz. shop-bought prepared and seasoned sausagemeat

2 tablespoons plain/all-purpose flour (gluten-free, if you wish)

1 egg, beaten

130 g/1¾ cups dried breadcrumbs (gluten-free if you wish; see page 9)

chutney, to serve

**SERVES 3**

A staple for any picnic, this portable dish is perfectly crispy on the outside with lip-smackingly tasty sausagemeat and egg on the inside.

Peel the eggs. Divide the sausagemeat into 3 equal portions using wet hands. Flatten each into a thin layer, then lay the egg in the centre and wrap the sausagemeat around. Roll each round in the flour, then dip in the beaten egg, shaking off any excess as you go, then into the breadcrumbs. Make sure each one is covered in the breadcrumbs all over.

Preheat the air-fryer to 180°C/350°F.

Add the scotch eggs to the preheated air-fryer and air-fry for 14 minutes (no need to turn during cooking). Eat either hot or cold, with some chutney on the side.

# CHEESE SCONES

½ teaspoon baking powder

210 g/1½ cups self-raising/self-rising flour (gluten-free if you wish), plus extra for dusting

50 g/3½ tablespoons cold butter, cubed

125 g/1½ cups grated mature Cheddar

a pinch of cayenne pepper

a pinch of salt

100 ml/7 tablespoons milk, plus extra for brushing the tops of the scones

**MAKES 12**

A lovely quick way to make a small batch of cheese scones. They're best eaten warm.

Mix the baking powder with the flour in a bowl, then add the butter and rub into the flour to form a crumblike texture. Add the cheese, cayenne pepper and salt and stir. Then add the milk, a little at a time, and bring together into a ball of dough.

Dust your work surface with flour. Roll the dough flat until about 1.5 cm/⅝ in. thick. Cut out the scones using a 6-cm/2½-in. diameter cookie cutter. Gather the offcuts into a ball, re-roll and cut more scones – you should get about 12 scones from the mixture. Place the scones on an air-fryer liner or a piece of pierced parchment paper.

Preheat the air-fryer to 180°C/350°F.

Add the scones to the preheated air-fryer and air-fry for 8 minutes, turning them over halfway to cook the other side. Remove and allow to cool a little, then serve warm.

# PITTA PIZZA

2 round wholemeal pitta breads
3 tablespoons passata/strained
    tomatoes
4 tablespoons grated mozzarella
1 teaspoon dried oregano
1 teaspoon olive oil
basil leaves, to serve

**SERVES 2**

A great use of round pitta breads as a pizza base,
this light meal can be made in minutes.

Preheat the air-fryer to 200°C/400°F.

Pop the pittas into the preheated air-fryer and air-fry
for 1 minute.

Remove the pittas from the air-fryer and spread a layer
of the passata/strained tomatoes on the pittas, then
scatter over the mozzarella, oregano and oil. Return to the
air-fryer and air-fry for a further 4 minutes. Scatter over
the basil leaves and serve immediately.

# WHOLEGRAIN PITTA CHIPS

2 round wholegrain pittas,
    chopped into quarters
1 teaspoon olive oil
½ teaspoon garlic salt

**SERVES 2**

These are great to serve with Muhammara (see
page 35), Tzatziki (see page 51) or Baba Ganoush (see
page 35). Ideally use oil in a spray bottle, but you can
brush it on using a pastry brush if you wish.

Preheat the air-fryer to 180°C/350°F.

Spray or brush each pitta quarter with olive oil and
sprinkle with garlic salt. Place in the preheated air-fryer
and air-fry for 4 minutes, turning halfway through cooking.
Serve immediately.

# MEAT

# ALL-DAY BREAKFAST

1 medium tomato, sliced in half
1 large flat mushroom, thickly
  sliced
2 slices bacon
2 eggs (whole and in their shells)
tomato ketchup, to serve
hot buttered toast (see page 10),
  to serve

**SERVES 1**

Possibly the laziest meal for one you can prepare in an air-fryer! It's a great way to impress others when they ask 'What does an air-fryer do?'.

Preheat the air-fryer to 180°C/350°F.

Add the tomato halves to the preheated air-fryer and air-fry for 3 minutes. Add all other ingredients and cook for a further 6 minutes.

Serve everything together, with the eggs in egg cups. Add a generous dollop of tomato ketchup and hot buttered toast if you wish.

# HONEY & MUSTARD SAUSAGES WITH POTATOES, PEPPERS & ONIONS

**400 g/14 oz. baby new potatoes**
**1 onion, chopped into 4 wedges**
**1 tablespoon olive oil**
**1 tablespoon runny honey**
**1 tablespoon wholegrain mustard**
**6 sausages**
**5 baby (bell) peppers, roughly chopped**
**salt and freshly ground black pepper**
**fresh rosemary sprigs, to garnish**

**SERVES 2**

A perfectly delicious combination – the saltiness of sausages combines beautifully with the sweetness of honey and piquancy of mustard. The potatoes, peppers and onions complement these flavours well.

Preheat the air-fryer to 180°C/350°F.

Chop any larger potatoes to 3 cm/1¼ in. in length (leave any smaller potatoes whole). Toss the potatoes and onion wedges in the oil with salt and pepper to taste. Add the potatoes and onion wedges to the preheated air-fryer and air-fry for 10 minutes.

Meanwhile, mix together the honey and mustard, then toss the sausages in the honey-mustard mixture until evenly covered. Add these to the air-fryer and cook for a further 6 minutes. Toss the food in the air-fryer and add the (bell) peppers, stir everything well and air-fry for a further 7 minutes. Tip on to a serving platter, garnish with fresh rosemary sprigs if you wish and serve.

# MINI MOROCCAN LAMB BURGERS

400 g/14 oz. minced/ground
   lamb
1 tablespoon freshly chopped
   coriander/cilantro
1 teaspoon freshly chopped mint
1/2 teaspoon smoked paprika
1 teaspoon ground cumin
1 tablespoon harissa paste
tzatziki (see page 51), to serve
pitta breads and salad leaves,
   to serve

**SERVES 2**

These moist little lamb burgers make for a delicious Mediterranean-style light bite with pitta bread, tzatziki and salad.

Combine all the ingredients in a food processor, then divide into 6 equal portions and mould into burgers.

Preheat the air-fryer to 180°C/350°F.

Add the burgers to the preheated air-fryer and air-fry for 9 minutes, turning halfway through cooking. Check the internal temperature of the burgers has reached at least 75°C/170°F using a meat thermometer – if not, cook for another few minutes. Serve tucked into warmed pitta breads, with salad leaves and tzatziki.

# APRICOT LAMB BURGERS

500 g/1 lb. 2 oz. minced/ground
   lamb
50 g/1/3 cup dried apricots,
   finely chopped
1 teaspoon ground cumin
1/2 teaspoon ground coriander
3/4 teaspoon salt
1 egg, beaten

**SERVES 4**

Dried apricots add a sweet and tangy moistness to these lamb burgers , giving them a wonderful Middle Eastern flavour.

Combine all the ingredients together in a food processor, then divide into 4 equal portions and mould into burgers.

Preheat the air-fryer to 180°C/350°F.

Add the burgers to the preheated air-fryer and air-fry for 15 minutes, turning carefully halfway through cooking. Check the internal temperature of the burgers has reached 75°C/170°F using a meat thermometer – if not, cook for another few minutes and then serve.

# GARLIC & PEPPER PORK CHOPS

2 x 250-g/9-oz. pork chops
1 tablespoon olive oil
garlic salt and freshly ground
    black pepper

**SERVES 2**

These moist and well-seasoned pork chops are pure comfort food! Great served with buttered new potatoes, green veg and mayonnaise.

Preheat the air-fryer to 180°C/350°F.

Rub the olive oil into each side of the chops, then season both sides with garlic salt and pepper.

Add the chops to the preheated air-fryer and air-fry for 10 minutes, turning them over after 4 minutes. Check the internal temperature of the chops has reached at least 63°C/145°F using a meat thermometer – if not, cook for another few minutes and then serve.


# HERBY LAMB CHOPS

8 lamb chops
1 teaspoon dried oregano
1 tablespoon olive oil
salt and freshly ground black
    pepper

**SERVES 4**

So simple to prepare and cook, lamb chops flavoured with oregano make an ideal meat feast.

Drizzle the oil over both sides of the chops and season both sides with the oregano, salt and pepper (a good dose of both). Leave to marinate for 30 minutes at room temperature.

Preheat the air-fryer to 180°C/350°F.

Add the chops to the preheated air-fryer and air-fry for 5–7 minutes, turning once during cooking. Check the internal temperature of the chops has reached at least 55°C/130°F using a meat thermometer – if not, cook for another few minutes and then serve.

# BEEF ADANA KEBABS

These aromatic Turkish kebabs are deliciously moist and perfect with tzatziki and a salad or served in a wrap.

1 onion, roughly chopped
1 baby red pepper or ½ a red (bell) pepper, roughly chopped
2 plump garlic cloves, chopped
½ teaspoon chilli/hot red pepper flakes
1 teaspoon ground cumin
1 teaspoon salt
3 tablespoons freshly chopped flat-leaf parsley
50 g/generous ½ cup dried breadcrumbs (gluten-free if you wish; see page 9)
500 g/1 lb. 2 oz. minced/ground beef
wraps or pitta breads, to serve
chopped cucumber and tomatoes and fresh mint leaves, to serve

## TZATZIKI

½ cucumber
250 g/1 generous cup Greek yogurt
1 garlic clove, finely chopped
2 teaspoons freshly chopped dill
2 teaspoons freshly squeezed lemon juice
sea salt, to taste

## SERVES 4

In a food processor whizz the onion, pepper and garlic to form a paste. Stir in the chilli/hot red pepper flakes, cumin, salt and then the parsley, breadcrumbs and beef. Divide the mixture into 6 equal portions, then roll into sausage shapes. Place in the fridge for at least 1 hour.

To make the tzatziki, place a paper towel or a clean dish towel on a chopping board and coarsely grate the cucumber directly onto the towel. Cover the cucumber with another paper towel or dish towel and flip it over (to remove some of the moisture), then remove the wet towel from the top. Give the cucumber a good sprinkle of sea salt.

In a medium bowl, combine the yogurt, garlic, dill and lemon juice. Add the cucumber to the yogurt mix. Give it a good stir and leave in the fridge for 30 minutes before serving.

Preheat the air-fryer to 180°C/350°F.

Thread each kebab onto a metal skewer. Add the kebabs to the preheated air-fryer and air-fry for 10–12 minutes, carefully rolling over the kebabs halfway through cooking. Check the internal temperature of the kebabs has reached at least 70°C/160°F using a meat thermometer – if not, cook for another few minutes. Serve the kebabs with the tzatziki alongside.

# MEDITERRANEAN BEEF MEATBALLS

500 g/1 lb. 2 oz. minced/ground
    beef
30 g/¹⁄₂ cup fresh breadcrumbs
    (gluten-free if you wish)
1 egg
1 teaspoon dried thyme
³⁄₄ teaspoon salt
¹⁄₂ teaspoon freshly ground black
    pepper
Mediterranean Sauce (see
    page 102) or 400-g/14-oz. jar
    tomato-based pasta sauce
spaghetti, basil leaves and freshly
    grated Parmesan, to serve

**SERVES 3**

A firm family favourite, moist herby meatballs are accompanied by a sweet and tangy tomato sauce.

Combine all the ingredients (not the sauce) together in a bowl, then divide into 9 equal portions and mould into meatballs.

Preheat the air-fryer to 180°C/350°F.

Place the meatballs in the preheated air-fryer and air-fry for 8 minutes, turning halfway through cooking.

Pour the sauce into a baking dish or gratin dish that fits into your air-fryer. After 8 minutes, pop the meatballs into the sauce in the dish and put the whole dish back into the air-fryer. Cook for a further 5 minutes, then check the internal temperature of the meatballs has reached at least 70°C/160°F using a meat thermometer – if not, cook for another few minutes.

Serve the meatballs piled on top of spaghetti, garnished with basil leaves and scattered with grated Parmesan.

# LAMB KOFTAS

600 g/1 lb. 5 oz. minced/ground
    lamb
1 onion, finely chopped
1 garlic clove, finely chopped
2 tablespoons finely chopped
    coriander/cilantro
1 teaspoon ground coriander
1 teaspoon ground cumin
1 teaspoon ground turmeric
¹⁄₂ teaspoon chilli/chili powder
1 teaspoon dried thyme
1 teaspoon salt
1 tablespoon runny honey

**SERVES 3**

These hearty and flavoursome kofta kebabs are wonderfully moist and ideal for air-fryer cooking. Great served with a Greek salad.

Combine all the ingredients in a bowl and mix together well. Divide into 6 equal portions and mould into sausage shapes. Place in the fridge for at least an hour before cooking.

Preheat the air-fryer to 180°C/350°F.

Thread a small metal skewer through each kofta. Place in the preheated air-fryer and air-fry for 10 minutes, turning halfway through cooking. Check the internal temperature of the koftas has reached at least 70°C/160°F using a meat thermometer – if not, cook for another few minutes and then serve.

# PORK SCHNITZEL

4 x 100-g/3½-oz. pork loin
    medallions
4 tablespoons plain/all-purpose
    flour (gluten-free if you wish)
½ teaspoon dried sage
¼–½ teaspoon salt (depending
    on taste)
¼ teaspoon freshly ground
    black pepper
2 eggs
100 g/1¾ cups fresh
    breadcrumbs
1 tablespoon olive oil
hasselback potatoes (see
    page 123), apple slices and
    green vegetables, to serve

**SERVES 4**

This is a decidedly easy way to make this great-tasting traditional German dish. It's perfect served with air-fried hasselback potatoes and apple slices or even a spoonful of sauerkraut.

Place the pork medallions in a plastic bag, one at a time, and bash with the end of a rolling pin or a meat tenteriser until you have thin escalopes (no thicker than 5 mm/¼ in.).

Mix the flour, sage, salt and pepper together in a shallow bowl. Beat the eggs in another shallow bowl. Place the breadcrumbs in a third shallow bowl.

Dip the pork escalopes in the seasoned flour. Next dip them in the egg, then in the breadcrumbs. Ensure they are coated with breadcrumbs all over.

Preheat the air-fryer to 180°C/350°F.

Place the escalopes in the preheated air-fryer on an air-fryer liner or a piece of pierced parchment paper. Drizzle over about ½ tablespoon olive oil. Air-fry for 3 minutes, then turn, drizzle over the remaining olive oil and cook for a further 3 minutes.

Check the internal temperature of the pork has reached at least 63°C/145°F using a meat thermometer – if not, cook for another few minutes and then serve with the potatoes, apple slices and green vegetables.

# TERIYAKI STEAK SKEWERS

4 sirloin steaks, diced into
   2.5-cm/1-in. cubes
sliced red chilli/chili, spring onion/
   scallion and coriander/cilantro,
   to garnish

## MARINADE

60 ml/4 tablespoons soy sauce
   (or tamari)
2 tablespoons runny honey
1 teaspoon unrefined sugar
½ teaspoon brown rice vinegar
½ teaspoon onion granules
1½ teaspoons freshly grated
   ginger
1½ teaspoons freshly grated
   garlic

**SERVES 4**

This Japanese-style marinade brings out the natural sweetness of the cubed steak. The steak not only has great flavour, but a melt-in-the-mouth texture too.

Make up the marinade by combining all ingredients in a jar and shaking vigorously.

Bring the steaks out of the fridge 30 minutes before cooking. Place in a bowl, cover with the marinade and leave to marinate at room temperature for the full 30 minutes.

Preheat the air-fryer to 180°C/350°F.

Thread the marinated steak pieces onto metal skewers and place these into the preheated air-fryer. Air-fry for 3–5 minutes, depending on how rare you like your steak. Serve immediately, scattered with sliced chilli/chili, spring onion/scallion and coriander/cilantro.

# SIMPLE STEAKS

2 x 220-g/8-oz. sirloin steaks
2 teaspoons olive oil
salt and freshly ground
   black pepper

**SERVES 2**

There are so many ways to cook a steak, but I think this is possibly the simplest I have ever used. The resulting steaks are deliciously tender.

Bring the steaks out of the fridge an hour before cooking. Drizzle with the oil, then rub with salt and pepper on both sides. Leave to marinate at room temperature for 1 hour.

Preheat the air-fryer to 180°C/350°F.

Add the steaks to the preheated air-fryer and air-fry for 5 minutes on one side, then turn and cook for a further 4 minutes on the other side (for medium rare). Check the internal temperature of the steak has reached 58°C/135°F using a meat thermometer – if not, cook for another few minutes. Leave to rest for a few minutes before serving.

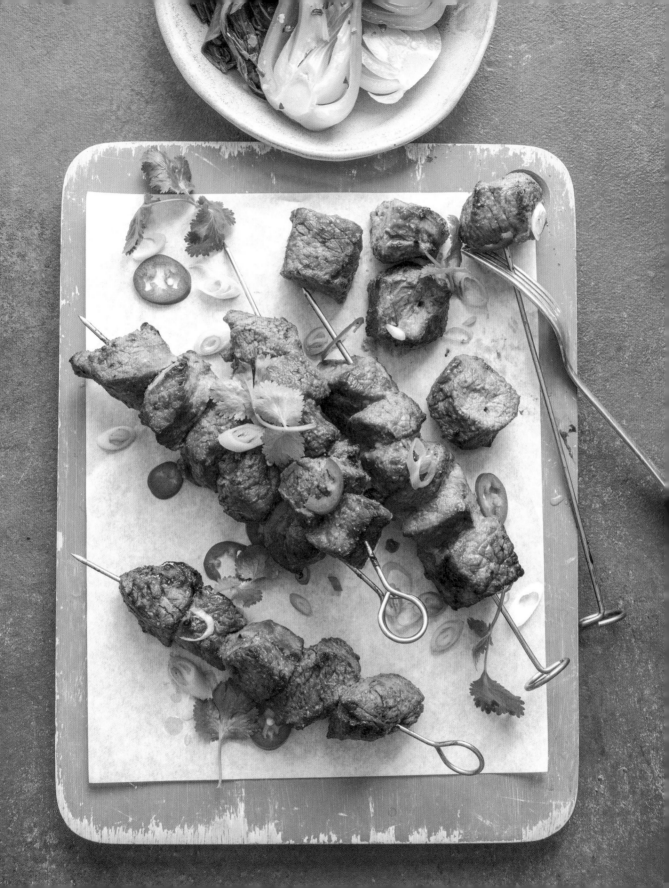

# POULTRY

# CHICKEN FAJITAS

2 boneless chicken breasts, sliced into strips

5 mini (bell) peppers, sliced into strips

1 courgette/zucchini, sliced into 5-mm/¼-in. thick discs

2 tablespoons olive oil

28-g/1-oz. packet fajita seasoning mix

**TO SERVE**

wraps
sliced avocado
chopped tomato and red onion
grated Red Leicester cheese
plain yogurt
coriander/cilantro
lime wedges, for squeezing

**SERVES 3**

Fajitas seem to fall into the category of 'fun food', in that once the meat and vegetables are prepared the 'building' process can begin with your own personal choice of additions.

Combine the chicken, (bell) peppers, courgettes/zucchini and olive oil in a bowl. Add the fajita seasoning and stir to coat.

Preheat the air-fryer to 180°C/350°F.

Add the coated vegetables and chicken to the preheated air-fryer and air-fry for 12 minutes, shaking the drawer a couple of times during cooking. Check the internal temperature of the chicken has reached at least 74°C/165°F using a meat thermometer – if not, cook for another few minutes.

Serve immediately alongside the serving suggestions or your own choices of accompaniments.

# PIZZA CHICKEN NUGGETS

60 g/³⁄₄ cup dried breadcrumbs
(see page 9)
20 g/¹⁄₄ cup grated Parmesan
¹⁄₂ teaspoon dried oregano
¹⁄₄ teaspoon freshly ground black
pepper
150 g/²⁄₃ cup Mediterranean
sauce (see page 102) or
150 g/5¹⁄₂ oz. jarred tomato
pasta sauce (keep any leftover
sauce for serving)
400 g/14 oz. chicken fillets

**SERVES 2**

These Italian-inspired nuggets combine two favourite foods – pizza with chicken nuggets. They're tangy and sweet whilst also being wonderfully savoury.

Preheat the air-fryer to 180°C/350°F.

Combine the breadcrumbs, Parmesan, oregano and pepper in a bowl. Have the Mediterranean or pasta sauce in a separate bowl.

Dip each chicken fillet in the tomato sauce first, then roll in the breadcrumb mix until coated fully.

Add the breaded fillets to the preheated air-fryer and air-fry for 10 minutes. Check the internal temperature of the chicken has reached at least 74°C/165°F using a meat thermometer – if not, cook for another few minutes.

Serve with some additional sauce that has been warmed through.

# CORNFLAKE CHICKEN NUGGETS

100 g/4 cups cornflakes
  (gluten-free if you wish)
70 g/½ cup plus ½ tablespoon
  plain/all-purpose flour
  (gluten-free if you wish)
2 eggs, beaten
½ teaspoon salt
¼ teaspoon freshly ground
  black pepper
600 g/1 lb. 5 oz. mini chicken
  fillets

**SERVES 4**

This crunchy coating is slightly sweeter than that of a traditional nugget. Younger family members, as well as older members of course, will enjoy these.

Grind the cornflakes in a food processor to a crumb-like texture. Place the flour in one bowl and the beaten eggs in a second bowl; season both bowls with the salt and pepper. Coat each chicken fillet in flour, tapping off any excess. Next dip each flour-coated chicken fillet into the egg, then the cornflakes until fully coated.

Preheat the air-fryer to 180°C/350°F.

Add the chicken fillets to the preheated air-fryer (you may need to add the fillets in two batches, depending on the size of your air-fryer) and air-fry for 10 minutes, turning halfway through cooking. Check the internal temperature of the nuggets has reached at least 74°C/165°F using a meat thermometer – if not, cook for another few minutes and then serve.

### VARIATION: SIMPLE CHICKEN NUGGETS

For a simpler version, replace the crushed cornflakes with 90 g/1¼ cups dried breadcrumbs (see page 9). Prepare and air-fry in the same way.

# GRAIN-FREE CHICKEN KATSU

125 g/1¼ cups ground almonds
½ teaspoon salt
½ teaspoon garlic powder
½ teaspoon dried parsley
½ teaspoon freshly ground
    black pepper
¼ teaspoon onion powder
¼ teaspoon dried oregano
450 g/1 lb. mini chicken fillets
1 egg, beaten
oil, for spraying/drizzling
coriander/cilantro leaves,
    to serve

**SERVES 2**

## KATSU SAUCE

1 teaspoon olive oil or avocado oil
1 courgette/zucchini (approx.
    150 g/5 oz.), finely chopped
1 carrot (approx. 100 g/3½ oz.),
    finely chopped
1 onion (approx. 120 g/4½ oz.),
    finely chopped
1 eating apple (approx. 150 g/
    5 oz.), cored and finely chopped
1 teaspoon ground ginger
1 teaspoon ground turmeric
2 teaspoons ground cumin
2 teaspoons ground coriander
1½ teaspoons mild chilli/chili
    powder
1 teaspoon garlic powder
1½ tablespoons runny honey
1 tablespoon soy sauce
    (gluten-free if you wish)
700 ml/3 cups vegetable stock
    (700 ml/3 cups water with
    1½ stock cubes)

**SERVES 4**

As you've seen from other recipes, the air-fryer is great for cooking crispy, breadcrumb-covered foods, but this version of chicken katsu uses seasoned ground almonds instead. However, you could use breaded chicken fillets if you wish. The sauce with the fillets, whichever way they are coated, is a must. Also great served with steamed rice and pak choi.

First make the sauce. The easiest way to ensure all the vegetables and apple are finely chopped is to combine them in a food processor. Heat the oil in a large saucepan and sauté the finely chopped vegetables and apple for 5 minutes. Add all the seasonings, honey, soy sauce and stock and stir well, then bring to a simmer and simmer for 30 minutes.

Meanwhile, mix together the ground almonds, seasonings and spices. Dip each chicken fillet into the beaten egg, then into the almond-spice mix, making sure each fillet is fully coated. Spray the coated chicken fillets with olive oil (or simply drizzle over).

Preheat the air-fryer to 180°C/350°F.

Place the chicken fillets in the preheated air-fryer and air-fry for 10 minutes, turning halfway through cooking. Check the internal temperature of the chicken has reached at least 74°C/165°F using a meat thermometer – if not, cook for another few minutes.

Blend the cooked sauce in a food processor until smooth. Serve the chicken with the Katsu Sauce drizzled over (if necessary, reheat the sauce gently before serving) and scattered with coriander leaves. Any unused sauce can be frozen.

# SATAY CHICKEN SKEWERS

3 chicken breasts, chopped into
  3 x 3-cm/1¼ x 1¼-in. cubes

## MARINADE

200 ml/¾ cup canned coconut
  milk (including the thick part
  from the can)
1 plump garlic clove, finely
  chopped
2 teaspoons freshly grated ginger
2 tablespoons soy sauce
1 heaped tablespoon peanut
  butter
1 tablespoon maple syrup
1 tablespoon mild curry powder
1 tablespoon fish sauce

SERVES 4

Rich and peanutty in flavour, this satay marinade is a perfect match for succulent chicken breast pieces. Great served with the Lime-Almond Satay Sauce on page 87.

Mix the marinade ingredients thoroughly in a bowl, then toss in the chopped chicken and stir to coat thoroughly. Leave in the fridge to marinate for at least 4 hours.

Preheat the air-fryer to 190°C/375°F.

Thread the chicken onto 8 metal skewers. Add to the preheated air-fryer (you may need to cook these in two batches, depending on the size of your air-fryer). Air-fry for 10 minutes. Check the internal temperature of the chicken has reached at least 74°C/165°F using a meat thermometer – if not, cook for another few minutes and then serve.

# CHICKEN TIKKA

2 chicken breasts, diced

## FIRST MARINADE

freshly squeezed juice of
  ½ a lemon
1 tablespoon freshly grated ginger
1 tablespoon freshly grated garlic
a good pinch of salt

## SECOND MARINADE

100 g/½ cup Greek yogurt
½ teaspoon chilli powder
½ teaspoon chilli paste
½ teaspoon turmeric
½ teaspoon garam masala
1 tablespoon olive oil

SERVES 2

This recipe provides tender chicken pieces with the greatest flavour due to the two-stage marinating process.

Mix the ingredients for the first marinade together in a bowl, add in the chicken and stir to coat all the chicken pieces. Leave in the fridge to marinate for 20 minutes.

Combine the second marinade ingredients. Once the first marinade has had 20 minutes, add the second marinade to the chicken and stir well. Leave in the fridge for at least 4 hours.

Preheat the air-fryer to 180°C/350°F.

Thread the chicken pieces onto metal skewers that fit in your air-fryer. Add the skewers to the preheated air-fryer and air-fry for 10 minutes. Check the internal temperature of the chicken has reached at least 74°C/165°F using a meat thermometer – if not, cook for another few minutes and then serve.

# KOREAN CHICKEN WINGS

6 chicken wings
1 tablespoon olive oil
salt and freshly ground
   black pepper
finely sliced spring onion/scallion,
   to garnish

### GLAZE

2 tablespoons rice wine vinegar
1½ tablespoons soy sauce
1 tablespoon unrefined sugar
1 teaspoon freshly grated ginger
1 tablespoon gochugaru
   (Korean red pepper paste)

**SERVES 2**

You'll want to pick these up and nibble away at every last tasty morsel of chicken on these flavour-packed wings.

Preheat the air-fryer to 200°C/400°F.

Toss the chicken wings in the oil, then season with a little salt and pepper. Add these to the preheated air-fryer and air-fry for 10 minutes.

Meanwhile, add the glaze ingredients to a small saucepan and heat over a medium heat until reduced and the alcohol has burnt off. You'll know it is ready when you can stir the thickened glaze and you momentarily see the base of the pan.

After the 10 minutes, brush the reduced glaze onto the chicken wings and cook for a further 5 minutes. Check the internal temperature of the wings has reached at least 74°C/165°F using a meat thermometer – if not, cook for another few minutes. Serve sprinkled with spring onion/scallion.

# THAI TURKEY BURGERS

1 courgette/zucchini, about
   200 g/7 oz.
400 g/14 oz. minced/ground
   turkey breast
35 g/½ cup fresh breadcrumbs
   (gluten-free if you wish)
1 teaspoon Thai 7 spice seasoning
1 teaspoon salt
1 teaspoon olive oil

**SERVES 4**

The courgette/zucchini used here adds flavour and texture, but most importantly it creates deliciously moist burgers.

Coarsely grate the courgette/zucchini, then place in a piece of muslin/cheesecloth and squeeze out the water. Combine the grated courgette with all other ingredients except the olive oil, mixing together well. Divide the mixture into 4 equal portions and mould into burgers. Brush with oil.

Preheat the air-fryer to 190°C/375°C.

Add the turkey burgers to the preheated air-fryer and air-fry for 15 minutes, turning once halfway through cooking. Check the internal temperature of the burgers has reached at least 74°C/165°F using a meat thermometer – if not, cook for another few minutes and then serve.

# STICKY CHICKEN TIKKA DRUMSTICKS

12 chicken drumsticks

**MARINADE**
100 g/½ cup Greek yogurt
2 tablespoons tikka paste
2 teaspoons ginger preserve
freshly squeezed juice of
   ½ a lemon
¾ teaspoon salt

**SERVES 4**

This sweet, sticky yogurt-based marinade is a great way to bring even greater taste to already flavoursome drumsticks.

Make slices across each of the drumsticks with a sharp knife. Mix the marinade ingredients together in a bowl, then add the drumsticks. Massage the marinade into the drumsticks, then leave to marinate in the fridge overnight or for at least 6 hours.

Preheat the air-fryer to 200°C/400°F.

Lay the drumsticks on an air-fryer liner or a piece of pierced parchment paper. Place the paper and drumsticks in the preheated air-fryer. Air-fry for 6 minutes, then turn over and cook for a further 6 minutes. Check the internal temperature of the drumsticks has reached at least 75°C/167°F using a meat thermometer – if not, cook for another few minutes and then serve.

# CHICKEN MILANESE

130 g/1¾ cups dried breadcrumbs
   (gluten-free if you wish, see
   page 9)
50 g/⅔ cup grated Parmesan
1 teaspoon dried basil
½ teaspoon dried thyme
¼ teaspoon freshly ground
   black pepper
1 egg, beaten
4 tablespoons plain/all-purpose
   flour (gluten-free if you wish)
4 boneless chicken breasts

**SERVES 4**

'Milanese' simply means coating meat in egg and breadcrumbs and then cooking. Originally made using veal, this chicken version is more popular with younger palates.

Combine the breadcrumbs, cheese, herbs and pepper in a bowl. In a second bowl beat the egg, and in the third bowl have the plain/all-purpose flour. Dip each chicken breast first into the flour, then the egg, then the seasoned breadcrumbs.

Preheat the air-fryer to 180°C/350°F.

Add the breaded chicken breasts to the preheated air-fryer and air-fry for 12 minutes. Check the internal temperature of the chicken has reached at least 74°C/165°F using a meat thermometer – if not, cook for another few minutes.

# CHICKEN KIEV

4 boneless chicken breasts
4 tablespoons plain/all-purpose
   flour (gluten-free if you wish)
1 egg, beaten
130 g/2 cups dried breadcrumbs
   (gluten-free if you wish, see
   page 9)

**GARLIC BUTTER**

60 g/4 tablespoons salted butter,
   softened
1 large garlic clove, finely chopped

**SERVES 4**

Chicken Kiev is so easy in the air-fryer. The garlic butter
needs to be frozen, so make this in advance.

Mash together the butter and garlic. Form into a sausage shape,
then slice into 4 equal discs. Place in the freezer until frozen.

Make a deep horizontal slit across each chicken breast,
taking care not to cut through to the other side. Stuff the cavity
with a disc of frozen garlic butter. Place the flour in a shallow
bowl, the egg in another and the breadcrumbs in a third. Coat
each chicken breast first in flour, then egg, then breadcrumbs.

Preheat the air-fryer to 180°C/350°F.

Add the chicken Kievs to the preheated air-fryer and air-fry
for 12 minutes until cooked through. This is hard to gauge as the
butter inside the breast is not an indicator of doneness, so test
the meat in the centre with a meat thermometer – it should be
at least 75°C/167°F; if not, cook for another few minutes.

# WHOLE CHICKEN

1.5-kg/3¼-lb. chicken
2 tablespoons butter or
   coconut oil
salt and freshly ground
   black pepper

**SERVES 4**

The air-fryer is one of the quickest yet tastiest ways to cook
a whole chicken, resulting in crispy skin and moist chicken.

Place the chicken breast-side up and carefully insert the butter
or oil between the skin and the flesh of each breast. Season.

Preheat the air-fryer to 180°C/350°F. If the chicken hits the
heating element, remove the drawer to lower the chicken a level.

Add the chicken to the preheated air-fryer breast-side up.
Air-fry for 30 minutes, then turn over and cook for a further
10 minutes. Check the internal temperature with a meat
thermometer. If it is 75°C/167°F at the thickest part, remove
the chicken from the air-fryer and leave to rest for 10 minutes
before carving. If less than 75°C/167°F, continue to cook until
this internal temperature is reached and then allow to rest.

# FISH & SEAFOOD

# COD IN PARMA HAM

2 x 175–190-g/6–7-oz. cod fillets,
   skin removed
6 slices Parma ham or prosciutto
16 cherry tomatoes
60 g/2 oz. rocket/arugula

**DRESSING**

1 tablespoon olive oil
1½ teaspoons balsamic vinegar
garlic salt, to taste
freshly ground black pepper,
   to taste

**SERVES 2**

Salty Parma ham wrapped around sweet, juicy cod fillets is a wonderful contrast of flavours. This combination is ideal served with a simply dressed rocket/arugula and roasted tomato salad.

Preheat the air-fryer to 180°C/350°F.

Wrap each piece of cod snugly in 3 ham slices. Add the ham-wrapped cod fillets and the tomatoes to the preheated air-fryer and air-fry for 6 minutes, turning the cod halfway through cooking. Check the internal temperature of the fish has reached at least 60°C/140°F using a meat thermometer – if not, cook for another minute.

Meanwhile, make the dressing by combining all the ingredients in a jar and shaking well.

Serve the cod and tomatoes on a bed of rocket/arugula with the dressing poured over.

# SEA BASS WITH ASPARAGUS SPEARS

2 x 100-g/3½-oz. sea bass fillets
8 asparagus spears
2 teaspoons olive oil
salt and freshly ground
 black pepper
boiled new potatoes, to serve

## CAPER DRESSING

1½ tablespoons olive oil
grated zest and freshly squeezed
 juice of ½ lemon
1 tablespoon small, jarred capers
1 teaspoon Dijon mustard
1 tablespoon freshly chopped
 flat-leaf parsley

SERVES 2

This combination of fish and asparagus cooks in under 10 minutes. That's the perfect amount of time to assemble the delicious caper dressing.

Preheat the air-fryer to 180°C/350°F.

Prepare the fish and asparagus by brushing both with the olive oil and sprinkling over salt and pepper.

Add the asparagus to the preheated air-fryer and air-fry for 4 minutes, then turn the asparagus and add the fish to the air-fryer drawer. Cook for a further 4 minutes. Check the internal temperature of the fish has reached at least 60°C/140°F using a meat thermometer – if not, cook for another minute.

Meanwhile, make the dressing by combining all the ingredients in a jar and shaking well. Pour the dressing over the cooked fish and asparagus spears and serve with new potatoes.

# FISH IN FOIL

1 tablespoon avocado oil or olive
 oil, plus extra for greasing
1 tablespoon soy sauce (or tamari)
1½ teaspoons freshly grated
 garlic
1½ teaspoons freshly grated
 ginger
1 small red chilli/chile, finely
 chopped
2 skinless, boneless white fish
 fillets (about 350 g/12 oz. total
 weight)

SERVES 2

A simple cooking method that delivers great results. The combination of soy sauce, garlic, ginger and chilli/chile brings the fish to a different flavour level.

Mix the oil, soy sauce, garlic, ginger and chilli/chile together. Brush a little oil onto two pieces of foil, then lay the fish in the centre of the foil. Spoon the topping mixture over the fish. Wrap the foil around the fish to make a parcel, with a gap above the fish but shallow enough to fit in your air-fryer basket.

Preheat the air-fryer to 180°C/350°F.

Add the foil parcels to the preheated air-fryer and air-fry for 7–10 minutes, depending on the thickness of your fillets. The fish should just flake when a fork is inserted. Serve immediately.

# PESTO SALMON

4 x 150–175-g/5½–6-oz. salmon
  fillets
lemon wedges, to serve

**PESTO**

50 g/scant ½ cup toasted pine
  nuts
50 g/2 oz. fresh basil
50 g/⅔ cup grated Parmesan
  or Pecorino
100 ml/7 tablespoons olive oil

**SERVES 4**

Pesto is a wonderfully aromatic addition to these
succulent salmon fillets. The cheese and pine nuts
combined with basil and oil totally deliver on taste.

To make the pesto, blitz the pine nuts, basil and Parmesan
to a paste in a food processor. Pour in the olive oil and
process again.

Preheat the air-fryer to 160°C/325°F.

Top each salmon fillet with 2 tablespoons of the pesto.
Add the salmon fillets to the preheated air-fryer and
air-fry for 9 minutes. Check the internal temperature of
the fish has reached at least 63°C/145°F using a meat
thermometer – if not, cook for another few minutes.

# STORE-CUPBOARD FISHCAKES

400 g/14 oz. cooked potato –
  either mashed potato or the
  insides of jacket potatoes
  (see page 124)
2 x 150–200-g/5½–7-oz. cans
  fish, such as tuna or salmon,
  drained
2 eggs
¾ teaspoon salt
1 teaspoon dried parsley
½ teaspoon freshly ground
  black pepper
1 tablespoon olive oil
caper dressing (see page 79),
  to serve

**SERVES 3**

An ideal weekday supper when you've run out of fresh
ingredients and ideas! Made from simple staples you
are likely to have in your cupboards or fridge, these are
a welcome comfort when served with a crisp salad.

Mix the cooked potato, fish, eggs, salt, parsley and pepper
together in a bowl, then divide into 6 equal portions and
form into fishcakes. Drizzle the olive oil over both sides of
each fishcake.

Preheat the air-fryer to 180°C/350°F.

Add the fishcakes to the preheated air-fryer and air-fry
for 15 minutes, turning halfway through cooking. Serve with
salad and tartare sauce or Caper Dressing.

# CAJUN PRAWN SKEWERS

350 g/12 oz. king prawns/
jumbo shrimp

**MARINADE**

1 teaspoon smoked paprika
1 teaspoon unrefined sugar
1 teaspoon salt
½ teaspoon onion powder
½ teaspoon mustard powder
¼ teaspoon dried oregano
¼ teaspoon dried thyme
1 teaspoon white wine vinegar
2 teaspoons olive oil

**SERVES 2**

These sweet, spicy, salty and succulent prawns/shrimp are ideal as an appetizer because once they're prepared and left in their marinade, they can be ready in minutes.

Mix all the marinade ingredients together in a bowl. Mix the prawns/shrimp into the marinade and cover. Place in the fridge to marinate for at least an hour.

Preheat the air-fryer to 180°C/350°F.

Thread 4–5 prawns/shrimp on to each skewer (you should have enough for 4–5 skewers). Add the skewers to the preheated air-fryer and air-fry for 2 minutes, then turn the skewers and cook for a further 2 minutes. Check the internal temperature of the prawns/shrimp has reached at least 50°C/125°F using a meat thermometer – if not, cook for another few minutes. Serve immediately.

# CRISPY CAJUN FISH FINGERS

350 g/12 oz. cod loins
1 teaspoon smoked paprika
½ teaspoon cayenne pepper
½ teaspoon onion granules
¾ teaspoon dried oregano
¼ teaspoon dried thyme
½ teaspoon salt
½ teaspoon unrefined sugar
40 g/½ cup dried breadcrumbs
    (gluten-free if you wish, see
    page 9)
2 tablespoons plain/all-purpose
    flour (gluten-free if you wish)
1 egg, beaten

**SERVES 2**

This combination of seasonings lifts the humble fish finger/fish stick to a new level. Great flavour, and not too spicy for the younger palate either.

Slice the cod into 6 equal fish 'fingers'. Mix the spices, herbs, salt and sugar together, then combine with the breadcrumbs. Lay out three bowls: one with flour, one with beaten egg and one with the Cajun-spiced breadcrumbs. Dip each fish finger into the flour, then the egg, then the breadcrumbs until fully coated.

Preheat the air-fryer to 180°C/350°F.

Add the fish to the preheated air-fryer and air-fry for 6 minutes, until cooked inside. Check the internal temperature of the fish has reached at least 75°C/167°F using a meat thermometer – if not, cook for another few minutes.

# OAT & PARMESAN CRUSTED FISH FILLETS

20 g/⅓ cup fresh breadcrumbs
25 g/3 tablespoons oats
15 g/¼ cup grated Parmesan
1 egg
2 x 175-g/6-oz. white fish fillets,
  skin-on
salt and freshly ground
  black pepper

SERVES 2

This cheesy crumb topping is a healthier way to enjoy fish. Delicious served with a raw slaw and lemon wedges.

Preheat the air-fryer to 180°C/350°F.

Combine the breadcrumbs, oats and cheese in a bowl and stir in a pinch of salt and pepper. In another bowl beat the egg. Dip the fish fillets in the egg, then top with the oat mixture.

Add the fish fillets to the preheated air-fryer on an air-fryer liner or a piece of pierced parchment paper. Air-fry for 10 minutes. Check the fish is just flaking away when a fork is inserted, then serve immediately.

# PARMESAN-COATED FISH FINGERS

350 g/12 oz. cod loins
1 tablespoon grated Parmesan
40 g/½ cup dried breadcrumbs
  (gluten-free if you wish, see
  page 9)
1 egg, beaten
2 tablespoons plain/all-purpose
  flour (gluten free if you wish)

SERVES 2

Fish fingers/fish sticks are tasty, there's no denying that, but many shop-bought ones contain added ingredients. Making your own, and even better with just a hint of cheesiness in the crust, is so easy.

Slice the cod into 6 equal fish fingers/sticks.

Mix the Parmesan together with the breadcrumbs. Lay out three bowls: one with flour, one with beaten egg and the other with the Parmesan breadcrumbs. Dip each fish finger/stick first into the flour, then the egg and then the breadcrumbs until fully coated.

Preheat the air-fryer to 180°C/350°F.

Add the fish to the preheated air-fryer and air-fry for 6 minutes. Check the internal temperature of the fish has reached at least 75°C/167°F using a meat thermometer – if not, cook for another few minutes. Serve immediately.

# THAI-STYLE TUNA FISHCAKES

200 g/7 oz. cooked potato

145 g/5 oz. canned tuna, drained

60 g/1 cup canned sweetcorn/corn kernels (drained weight)

½ teaspoon soy sauce

½ teaspoon fish sauce

½ teaspoon Thai 7 spice

freshly squeezed juice of ½ a lime

1 teaspoon freshly grated garlic

1 teaspoon freshly grated ginger

avocado or olive oil, for brushing

## LIME-ALMOND SATAY SAUCE

20 ml/4 teaspoons fresh lime juice

2 heaped tablespoons almond butter

1 teaspoon soy sauce

½ teaspoon freshly grated ginger

½ teaspoon freshly grated garlic

½ teaspoon avocado or olive oil

½ teaspoon maple syrup

**SERVES 2**

These fishcakes deliver saltiness and sweetness and are extremely satisfying. The cooked potato can be mashed potato or the inside of a jacket potato (see page 124).

Combine all the fishcake ingredients in a food processor and blend together. Divide the mixture into 6 equal portions and mould into fishcakes. Brush a little oil over the top surface of the fishcakes.

Preheat the air-fryer to 180°C/350°F.

Place the fishcakes on an air-fryer liner or a piece of pierced parchment paper and add to the preheated air-fryer. Air-fry for 4 minutes, then turn over and brush the other side of each fishcake with oil and air-fry for a further 4 minutes.

To make the satay dipping sauce, mix all ingredients in a bowl with 1 tablespoon warm water. Serve alongside the fishcakes.

# GARLIC-PARSLEY PRAWNS

300 g/10½ oz. raw king prawns/jumbo shrimp (without shell)

40 g/3 tablespoons garlic butter, softened (see page 72)

2 tablespoons freshly chopped flat-leaf parsley

**SERVES 2**

Create succulent melt-in-the-mouth prawns/shrimp in a matter of minutes. This is fast food at its simplest and best.

Thread the prawns/shrimp onto 6 metal skewers that will fit your air-fryer. Mix together the softened garlic butter and parsley and brush evenly onto the prawn skewers.

Preheat the air-fryer to 180°C/350°F.

Place the skewers on an air-fryer liner or a piece of pierced parchment paper. Add the skewers to the preheated air-fryer and air-fry for 2 minutes, then turn the skewers over and cook for a further 2 minutes. Check the internal temperature of the prawns has reached at least 50°C/120°F using a meat thermometer – if not, cook for another few minutes and serve.

# VEGETARIAN & VEGAN

# QUINOA-STUFFED ROMANO PEPPERS

1 tablespoon olive oil
1 onion, diced
1 garlic clove, chopped
100 g/²/₃ cup uncooked quinoa
1½ tablespoons fajita seasoning
140 g/1 cup canned sweetcorn/
  corn kernels (drained weight)
3 romano peppers, sliced
  lengthways, seeds removed
  but stalk left intact
60 g/²/₃ cup grated mature
  Cheddar

**SERVES 2**

This spicy quinoa filling goes so well with the natural sweetness of the peppers.

Heat the oil in a saucepan. Add the onion and garlic and sauté for 5 minutes, until soft. Add the quinoa, fajita seasoning and 250 ml/1 cup water. Bring to a simmer, then cover with a lid and simmer for 15 minutes or until the quinoa is cooked and the water absorbed. Stir in the sweetcorn/corn kernels. Stuff each pepper half with the quinoa mixture, then top with grated cheese.

Preheat the air-fryer to 180°C/350°F.

Place the peppers on an air-fryer liner or a piece of pierced parchment paper, place in the preheated air-fryer and air-fry for 12–14 minutes, depending how 'chargrilled' you like your peppers.

# SATAY TOFU SKEWERS

300 g/10½ oz. firm tofu
Lime-Almond Satay Sauce (see
  page 87), to serve

**MARINADE**
200 ml/³/₄ cup coconut milk
  (including the thick part from
  the can)
1 plump garlic clove, finely
  chopped
2 teaspoons grated ginger
2 tablespoons soy sauce
1 heaped tablespoon smooth
  peanut butter
1 tablespoon maple syrup
1 tablespoon mild curry powder
1 tablespoon fish sauce or
  plant-based alternative

**SERVES 2**

The flavour imparted from the marinade is a great match for the taste and texture of the tofu itself. These skewers go so well with the Lime-Almond Satay Sauce on page 87.

Cut the tofu into 2 x 2-cm/¾ x ¾-in. cubes. Mix the marinade ingredients thoroughly, then toss in the tofu cubes. Once the tofu cubes are covered in the marinade, leave in the fridge to marinate for at least 4 hours.

Preheat the air-fryer to 180°C/350°F.

Thread the tofu cubes onto 4 skewers that fit inside your air-fryer. Place on an air-fryer liner or a piece of pierced parchment paper and add to the preheated air-fryer. Air-fry for 12 minutes, turning over once during cooking.

Serve the tofu skewers alongside a bowl of the Lime-Almond Satay Sauce.

# FLAT MUSHROOM PIZZAS

2 portobello mushrooms,
  cleaned and stalk removed
6 mozzarella balls
1 teaspoon olive oil

**PIZZA SAUCE**

100 g/3½ oz. passata/strained
  tomatoes
1 teaspoon dried oregano
¼ teaspoon garlic salt

**SERVES 1**

Cooking mushrooms in the air-fryer intensifies their wonderful flavour and succulence. The combination of mushroom with a simple pizza sauce and mozzarella brings a result that is far greater than the sum of its parts.

Preheat the air-fryer to 180°C/350°F.

Mix the ingredients for the pizza sauce together in a small bowl. Fill each upturned portobello mushroom with sauce, then top each with three mozzarella balls and drizzle the olive oil over.

Add the mushrooms to the preheated air-fryer and air-fry for 8 minutes. Serve immediately.

# TWO-STEP PIZZA

**BASE**

130 g/generous ½ cup Greek
  yogurt
125 g self-raising/self-rising flour,
  plus extra for dusting
¼ teaspoon salt

**PIZZA SAUCE**

100 g/3½ oz. passata/strained
  tomatoes
1 teaspoon dried oregano
¼ teaspoon garlic salt

**TOPPINGS**

75 g/2½ oz. mozzarella, torn
fresh basil leaves, to garnish

**SERVES 1**

What could be simpler than a two-step pizza? It's encouragingly easy, and once you've mastered this version, you can experiment with different toppings!

Mix together the base ingredients in a bowl. Once the mixture starts to look crumbly, use your hands to bring the dough together into a ball. Transfer to a piece of floured parchment paper and roll to about 5 mm/¼ in. thick. Transfer to a second piece of non-floured parchment paper.

Preheat the air-fryer to 200°C/400°F.

Meanwhile, mix the pizza sauce ingredients together in a small bowl and set aside.

Prick the pizza base all over with a fork and transfer (on the parchment paper) to the preheated air-fryer and air-fry for 5 minutes. Turn the pizza base over and top with the pizza sauce and the torn mozzarella. Cook for a further 3–4 minutes, until the cheese has melted. Serve immediately with the basil scattered over the top.

# AUBERGINE PARMIGIANA

2 small or 1 large aubergine/
    eggplant, sliced 5 mm/¼ in.
    thick
1 tablespoon olive oil
¾ teaspoon salt
200 g/7 oz. mozzarella, sliced
½ teaspoon freshly ground
    black pepper
20 g/¼ cup finely grated
    Parmesan
green vegetables, to serve

## SAUCE

135 g/5 oz. passata/strained
    tomatoes
1 teaspoon dried oregano
¼ teaspoon garlic salt
1 tablespoon olive oil

**SERVES 2 AS A MAIN
OR 4 AS A SIDE**

Air-fried aubergine/eggplant tastes delicious and is quick to cook. However, when combined with other ingredients to make this aubergine parmigiana, it's even more delicious!

Preheat the air-fryer to 200°C/400°F.

Rub each of the aubergine/eggplant slices with olive oil and salt. Divide the slices into two batches. Place one batch of the aubergine slices in the preheated air-fryer and air-fry for 4 minutes on one side, then turn over and air-fry for 2 minutes on the other side. Lay these on the base of a gratin dish that fits into your air-fryer.

Air-fry the second batch of aubergine slices in the same way. Whilst they're cooking, mix together the sauce ingredients in a small bowl.

Spread the sauce over the aubergines in the gratin dish. Add a layer of the mozzarella slices, then season with pepper. Add a second layer of aubergine slices, then top with Parmesan.

Place the gratin dish in the air-fryer and air-fry for 6 minutes, until the mozzarella is melted and the top of the dish is golden brown. Serve immediately with green vegetables on the side.

# GOAT'S CHEESE TARTLETS

1 readymade sheet of puff pastry, 35 x 23 cm/14 x 9 in. (gluten-free if you wish)

4 tablespoons pesto (jarred or see page 80)

4 roasted baby (bell) peppers (see page 120)

4 tablespoons soft goat's cheese

2 teaspoons milk (plant-based if you wish)

**SERVES 2**

Readymade puff pastry cooks so easily and quickly in an air-fryer. These tartlets are a wonderfully simple light lunch when you're short on time.

Cut the pastry sheet in half along the long edge, to make two smaller rectangles. Fold in the edges of each pastry rectangle to form a crust. Using a fork, prick a few holes in the base of the pastry. Brush half the pesto onto each rectangle, top with the peppers and goat's cheese. Brush the pastry crust with milk.

Preheat the air-fryer to 180°C/350°F.

Place one tartlet on an air-fryer liner or a piece of pierced parchment paper in the preheated air-fryer and air-fry for 6 minutes (you'll need to cook them one at a time). Repeat with the second tartlet.

# CHEESE, TOMATO & PESTO CRUSTLESS QUICHES

40 g/½ cup grated mature Cheddar

3 eggs, beaten

3 cherry tomatoes, finely chopped

salt and freshly ground black pepper

½ teaspoon olive oil, to grease ramekins

2 tablespoons pesto (jarred or see page 80)

**SERVES 1–2**

Perfect for breakfast or lunch, these quiches are great on their own or served with a salad.

Preheat the air-fryer to 180°C/350°F.

Mix together the cheese, eggs, tomatoes, salt and pepper in a bowl.

Grease the ramekins with the oil (and line with parchment paper if you wish to remove the quiches to serve). Pour the egg mixture into the ramekins.

Place the ramekins in the preheated air-fryer and air-fry for 10 minutes, stirring the contents of the ramekins halfway through cooking. Serve hot with 1 tablespoon pesto drizzled over each quiche.

# BAKED FETA, TOMATO & GARLIC PASTA

100 g/3½ oz. feta or plant-based feta, cubed
20 cherry tomatoes
2 garlic cloves, peeled and halved
¾ teaspoon oregano
1 teaspoon chilli/hot red pepper flakes
½ teaspoon garlic salt
2 tablespoons olive oil
100 g/3½ oz. cooked pasta plus about 1 tablespoon of cooking water
freshly ground black pepper

SERVES 2

A trend that recently took the internet by storm was a simple baked feta and tomato dish that made the simplest pasta sauce once cooked. This is my air-fryer version.

Preheat the air-fryer to 200°C/400°F.

Place the feta, tomatoes and garlic in a baking dish that fits inside your air-fryer. Top with the oregano, chilli/hot red pepper flakes, garlic salt and olive oil. Place the dish in the preheated air-fryer and air-fry for 10 minutes, then remove and stir in the pasta and cooking water. Serve sprinkled with black pepper.

# SAGANAKI

200 g/7 oz. kefalotyri or manouri cheese, sliced into wedges 1 cm/½ in. thick
2 tablespoons plain/all-purpose flour
olive oil, for drizzling

SERVES 2

Saganaki is the name given to a range of Greek dishes cooked in a small pan called a 'saganaki'. There are various cheeses you can choose to make this, such as kefalotyri cheese, which is a hard, salty cheese with a slightly piquant aftertaste. However, you can also use manouri, a by-product of feta production and slightly crumblier.

Preheat the air-fryer to 200°C/400°F.

Dip each wedge of cheese in the flour, then tap off any excess. Drizzle olive oil onto both sides of the cheese slices

Add the cheese to the preheated air-fryer and air-fry for 3 minutes. Remove from the air-fryer and serve.

# SHAKSHUKA

2 eggs

**BASE**

100 g/3½ oz. thinly sliced (bell) peppers

1 red onion, halved and thinly sliced

2 medium tomatoes, chopped

2 teaspoons olive oil

¼ teaspoon salt

¼ teaspoon freshly ground black pepper

½ teaspoon chilli/hot red pepper flakes

**SAUCE**

100 g/3½ oz. passata/strained tomatoes

1 tablespoon tomato purée/paste

1 teaspoon balsamic vinegar

½ teaspoon runny honey

½ teaspoon ground cumin

½ teaspoon paprika

¼ teaspoon salt

⅛ teaspoon freshly ground black pepper

**SERVES 2**

In this dish sweet peppers and onion in a tomato sauce combine so well with the creamy, just-cooked eggs.

Preheat the air-fryer to 180°C/350°F.

Combine the base ingredients together in a baking dish that fits inside your air-fryer. Add the dish to the preheated air-fryer and air-fry for 10 minutes, stirring halfway through cooking.

Meanwhile, combine the sauce ingredients in a bowl. Pour this into the baking dish when the 10 minutes are up. Stir, then make a couple of wells in the sauce for the eggs. Crack the eggs into the wells, then cook for a further 5 minutes or until the eggs are just cooked and yolks still runny. Remove from the air-fryer and serve.

# ARANCINI

300 g/10½ oz. leftover cold
  risotto
2 tablespoons plain/all-purpose
  flour (gluten-free if you wish)
1 egg, beaten
65 g/1 cup dried breadcrumbs
  (gluten-free if you wish, see
  page 9)
a few fresh basil leaves, to serve

## MEDITERRANEAN SAUCE

1 teaspoon olive oil
1 red (bell) pepper, chopped
1 onion, chopped
2 teaspoons chopped garlic
1 tablespoon tomato ketchup
  (can use a reduced sugar and
  salt version if you wish)
½ teaspoon salt
1 teaspoon dried oregano
150 ml/⅔ cup water
400-g/14-oz can chopped
  tomatoes

SERVES 2–3

The ideal way to use up leftovers, these arancini
can be prepared from any leftover risotto that has
been completely cooled and refrigerated.

To make the sauce, heat a saucepan over a medium
heat and add the oil. Once hot, add the (bell) pepper,
onion and garlic. Sauté for 5 minutes, then add all the
other ingredients and stir again. Bring to the boil, then
simmer for 15 minutes while you make the arancini.

Preheat the air-fryer to 180°C/350°F.

Divide the leftover risotto into 6 equal portions and
roll into balls. Create a line of bowls – one bowl with the
flour, one with the egg and one with the breadcrumbs.
Roll each ball in flour, then egg, then breadcrumbs until
fully coated.

Place these in the preheated air-fryer and air-fry
for 7 minutes. Check the internal temperature of the
arancini has reached 74°C/165°F using a meat
thermometer – if not, cook for another few minutes.
Serve with the Mediterranean sauce and scattered
with basil leaves.

# BUTTERNUT SQUASH FALAFEL

500 g/1 lb. 2 oz. frozen butternut
    squash cubes
1 tablespoon olive oil, plus extra
    for cooking
100 g/³/₄ cup canned or cooked
    chickpeas (drained weight)
20 g/¹/₄ cup gram/chickpea flour
1 teaspoon ground cumin
¹/₂ teaspoon ground coriander
¹/₂ teaspoon salt

**SERVES 2**

Cooking the butternut squash in your air-fryer first
and then adding it to the rest of the falafel ingredients
results in moister and sweeter pattie than the norm.
They lend themselves so well to being combined with
hummus and salad.

Preheat the air-fryer to 180°C/350°F.

Toss the frozen butternut squash in the olive oil. Add to the
preheated air-fryer and air-fry for 12–14 minutes, until soft but
not caramelized. Remove from the air-fryer and mash the
squash by hand or using a food processor, then combine with
the chickpeas, flour, spices and salt. Leave the mixture to cool,
then divide into 6 equal portions and mould into patties.

Preheat the air-fryer to 180°C/350°F.

Spray the patties with a little olive oil, then add to the
preheated air-fryer and air-fry for 10 minutes, turning once
(carefully) during cooking. Enjoy hot or cold.

# CHICKPEA FALAFEL

400-g/14-oz can chickpeas,
    drained and rinsed
3 tablespoons freshly chopped
    coriander/cilantro
1 plump garlic clove, chopped
freshly squeezed juice of
    ¹/₂ a lemon
1 teaspoon ground cumin
1 teaspoon smoked paprika
1 teaspoon salt
2 teaspoons olive oil (plus extra
    in a spray bottle or simply
    drizzle over)
¹/₂ teaspoon chilli/hot red pepper
    flakes

**SERVES 2**

These lightly spiced falafel are perfect served with
pittas, salad and a spoonful of tzatziki (see page 51).

In a food processor combine all the ingredients except the chilli/
hot red pepper flakes. Divide the mixture into 6 equal portions
and mould into patties.

Preheat the air-fryer to 180°C/350°F.

Spray each falafel with extra olive oil and sprinkle with chilli/
hot red pepper flakes, then place in the preheated air-fryer and
air-fry for 7 minutes, or until just brown on top. Remove carefully
and serve.

# MISO MUSHROOMS ON SOURDOUGH TOAST

1 teaspoon miso paste
1 teaspoon oil, such as avocado
   or coconut (melted)
1 teaspoon soy sauce
80 g/3 oz. chestnut mushrooms,
   sliced 5 mm/$^1$/2 in. thick
1 large slice sourdough bread
2 teaspoons butter or plant-
   based spread
a little freshly chopped flat-leaf
   parsley, to serve

**SERVES 1**

This is a dish packed full of comforting umami-rich flavours and textures. It can easily be scaled up to serve two, but you might just need to cook the toast after the mushrooms, depending on the size of your air-fryer.

Preheat the air-fryer to 200°C/400°F.

In a small bowl or ramekin mix together the miso paste, oil and soy sauce.

Place the mushrooms in a small shallow gratin dish that fits inside your air-fryer. Add the sauce to the mushrooms and mix together. Place the gratin dish in the preheated air-fryer and air-fry for 6–7 minutes, stirring once during cooking.

With 4 minutes left to cook, add the bread to the air-fryer and turn over at 2 minutes whilst giving the mushrooms a final stir.

Once cooked, butter the toast and serve the mushrooms on top, scattered with chopped parsley.

# BAKED AUBERGINE SLICES
# WITH YOGURT DRESSING

1 aubergine/eggplant, sliced
   1.5 cm/⁵/₈ in. thick
3 tablespoons olive oil
½ teaspoon salt

**YOGURT DRESSING**

1 small garlic clove
1 tablespoon tahini or nut butter
100 g/½ cup Greek yogurt
2 teaspoons freshly squeezed
   lemon juice
1 tablespoon runny honey
a pinch of salt
a pinch of ground cumin
a pinch of sumac

**TO SERVE**

30 g/1 oz. rocket/arugula
2 tablespoons freshly chopped
   mint
3 tablespoons pomegranate
   seeds

**SERVES 2**

Soft and buttery cooked aubergine/eggplant is simply delicious served with this Middle Eastern-inspired yogurt dressing.

Preheat the air-fryer to 180°C/350°F.

Drizzle the olive oil over each side of the aubergine/eggplant slices. Sprinkle with salt. Add the aubergines to the preheated air-fryer and air-fry for 10 minutes, turning halfway through cooking.

Meanwhile, make the dressing by combining all the ingredients in a mini food processor (alterantively, finely chop the garlic, add to a jar with the other ingredients and shake vigorously).

Serve the cooked aubergine slices on a bed of rocket/arugula, drizzled with the dressing and with the mint and pomegranate seeds scattered over the top.

# SIDE DISHES

# CRISPY BROCCOLI

170 g/6 oz. broccoli florets
2 tablespoons olive oil
1/8 teaspoon garlic salt
1/8 teaspoon freshly ground
  black pepper
2 tablespoons freshly grated
  Parmesan or Pecorino

**SERVES 2**

These crispy, cheesy broccoli florets are unbelievably flavoursome, and such an easy side dish to prepare.

Preheat the air-fryer to 200°C/400°F.

Toss the broccoli in the oil, season with the garlic salt and pepper, then toss over the grated cheese and combine well. Add the broccoli to the preheated air-fryer and air-fry for 5 minutes, giving the broccoli a stir halfway through to ensure even cooking.

# CRISPY SWEET & SPICY CAULIFLOWER

1/2 a head of cauliflower
1 teaspoon sriracha sauce
1 teaspoon soy sauce (or tamari)
1/2 teaspoon maple syrup
2 teaspoons olive oil or
  avocado oil

**SERVES 2**

These lightly spiced cauliflower florets are ideal for adding to a nourish bowl.

Preheat the air-fryer to 180°C/350°F.

Chop the cauliflower into florets with a head size of roughly 2.5 cm/1 in. Place the other ingredients in a bowl and mix together, then add the florets and toss to coat them.

Add the cauliflower to the preheated air-fryer and air-fry for 12 minutes, shaking the drawer a couple of times during cooking.

# HONEY ROASTED PARSNIPS

350 g/12 oz. parsnips
1 tablespoon plain/all-purpose
 flour (gluten-free if you wish)
1½ tablespoons runny honey
2 tablespoons olive oil
salt

SERVES 4

A comforting dish for the cooler months.

Top and tail the parsnips, then slice lengthways, about
2 cm/¾ in. wide. Place in a saucepan with water to cover
and a good pinch of salt. Bring to the boil, then boil for
5 minutes.

Remove and drain well, allowing any excess water to
evaporate. Dust the parsnips with flour. Mix together the
honey and oil in a small bowl, then toss in the parsnips to
coat well in the honey and oil.

Preheat the air-fryer to 180°C/350°F.

Add the parsnips to the preheated air-fryer and air-fry
for 14–16 minutes, depending on how dark you like the
outsides (the longer you cook them, the sweeter they get).

# ROASTED BRUSSELS SPROUTS

300 g/10½ oz. Brussels sprouts,
 trimmed and halved
1 tablespoon olive oil
½ teaspoon salt
¼ teaspoon freshly ground
 black pepper

SERVES 3

Love them or hate them, you should try this air-
fried version before you really decide. They're crispy
and sweet and a world apart from the over-boiled,
soggy sprouts you may remember as a child.

Preheat the air-fryer to 160°C/325°F.

Toss the Brussels sprout halves in the oil and the
seasoning. Add these to the preheated air-fryer and
air-fry for 15 minutes, then increase the temperature
of the air-fryer to 180°C/350°F and cook for a further
5 minutes until the sprouts are really crispy on the outside
and cooked through.

# BUTTERNUT SQUASH

500 g/1 lb. 2 oz. butternut
   squash, chopped into
   2.5-cm/1-in. cubes
1 tablespoon olive oil or
   avocado oil
1 teaspoon smoked paprika
1 teaspoon dried oregano
½ teaspoon salt
¼ teaspoon freshly ground
   black pepper

**SERVES 4**

These cubes of butternut squash cook beautifully in the air-fryer and the light seasoning makes them tasty and versatile. Use in salads (great with lettuce and feta cheese), on top of tartlets or in a wrap.

Preheat the air-fryer to 180°C/350°F.

In a bowl toss the butternut squash cubes in the oil and all the seasonings.

Add the butternut squash cubes to the preheated air-fryer and air-fry for 16–18 minutes, shaking the drawer once during cooking.

# ASPARAGUS SPEARS

1 bunch of trimmed asparagus
1 teaspoon olive oil
¼ teaspoon salt
⅛ teaspoon freshly ground
   black pepper

**SERVES 2**

One of the quickest ways to cook asparagus to your personal liking. Try serving them with a soft-boiled/soft-cooked egg (see page 10).

Preheat the air-fryer to 180°C/350°F.

Toss the asparagus spears in the oil and seasoning. Add these to the preheated air-fryer and air-fry for 8–12 minutes, turning once (cooking time depends on the thickness of the stalks, which should retain some bite).

# MEDITERRANEAN VEGETABLES

1 courgette/zucchini, thickly
   sliced
1 (bell) pepper, deseeded and
   chopped into large chunks
1 red onion, sliced into wedges
12 cherry tomatoes
1 tablespoon olive oil
½ teaspoon salt
½ teaspoon freshly ground
   black pepper
2 rosemary twigs
mozzarella, fresh pesto (see
   page 80) and basil leaves,
   to serve

SERVES 1–2

When you hear about the health benefits of 'eating a rainbow' (of vegetables) each day, it sometimes feels overwhelming but a plate of deliciously sweet roasted Mediterranean vegetables makes this easily achievable.

Preheat the air-fryer to 180°C/350°F.

Toss the prepared vegetables in the oil and seasoning. Add the vegetables and the rosemary to the preheated air-fryer and air-fry for 12–14 minutes, depending on how 'chargrilled' you like them.

Remove and serve topped with fresh mozzarella and pesto and scattered with basil leaves.

# PATATAS BRAVAS

750 g/1 lb. 10 oz. baby new
    potatoes
1 tablespoon olive oil
¼ teaspoon salt
freshly chopped flat-leaf parsley,
    to garnish

**SAUCE**

1 tablespoon olive oil
1 small red onion, finely diced
2–3 garlic cloves, crushed
1 tablespoon smoked paprika
¼ teaspoon cayenne pepper
400-g/14-oz. can chopped
    tomatoes
4 pitted green olives, halved
½ teaspoon salt

**SERVES 4**

A staple in any tapas bar and an ideal accompaniment
to many a meal. Whilst the potatoes are easily cooked
using the air-fryer, the sauce elevates this side dish to
another level.

Preheat the air-fryer to 200°C/400°F.

Rinse the potatoes and chop them to the same size as the
smallest potato, then toss in the olive oil and sprinkle with the
salt. Place the potatoes in the preheated air-fryer and air-fry
for 18 minutes. Toss or shake the potatoes in the drawer
halfway through.

While the potatoes are cooking, make the sauce. Heat the
olive oil in a saucepan over a medium heat. Add the onion and
sauté for about 5 minutes. Add the garlic, paprika and cayenne
and cook for 1 minute. Add the tomatoes, olives and salt, plus
125 ml/½ cup water and simmer for about 20 minutes, until
thickened. Purée the sauce in a blender or food processor.

Serve the potatoes in a bowl with the sauce poured over
and the chopped parsley scattered over the top.

# SWEET & SPICY BABY PEPPERS

200 g/7 oz. piccarella (baby)
    peppers, deseeded and
    quartered lengthways
1 teaspoon olive oil
½ teaspoon chilli/chili paste
¼ teaspoon runny honey
salt and freshly ground
    black pepper

**SERVES 2**

These mini peppers are so versatile. Serve them as
a tasty side dish or try them as a filling for tartlets
(see page 97) or a topping for pasta dishes.

Preheat the air-fryer to 180°C/350°F.

Toss the peppers in the oil, chilli/chili paste and honey, then
add salt and pepper to taste.

Place in the preheated air-fryer and air-fry for 6–8 minutes,
depending on how 'chargrilled' you like them, turning them over
halfway through.

# HASSELBACK NEW POTATOES

8–12 new potatoes, roughly
    5–7 cm/2–2¾ in. in length
2 teaspoons olive oil
salt
1 tablespoon butter (optional)

**SERVES 4**

New potatoes are perfect for these small hasselback potatoes. They not only look great, but the oil and salt permeate into the fine slices of each potato to really bring out the great taste of the new potatoes.

Preheat the air-fryer to 180°C/350°F.

Slice the potatoes multiple times widthways, making sure you do not cut all the way through (if you place the potatoes in the bowl of a wooden spoon to make these slices, it prevents you cutting all the way through). Coat the potatoes in the olive oil and sprinkle over the salt.

Add the potatoes to the preheated air-fryer and air-fry for 20–25 minutes until the potatoes are crispy on the outside but soft on the inside. Serve immediately.

# YORKSHIRE PUDDINGS

1 tablespoon olive oil
70 g/½ cup plus ½ tablespoon
    plain/all-purpose flour
    (gluten-free if you wish)
100 ml/7 tablespoons milk
2 eggs
salt and freshly ground
    black pepper

**SERVES 2**

An ideal recipe for cooking a small quantity of Yorkshire puddings/popovers, either for a roast dinner or as a lunch alternative to bread. Crispy outside and fluffy inside, they're great filled with smoked fish.

You will need 4 ramekins. Preheat the air-fryer to 200°C/400°F.

Using a pastry brush, oil the base and sides of each ramekin, dividing the oil equally between the ramekins. Place the greased ramekins in the preheated air-fryer and heat for 5 minutes.

Meanwhile, in a food processor or using a whisk, combine the flour, milk, eggs and seasoning until you have a batter that is frothy on top. Divide the batter equally between the preheated ramekins. Return the ramekins to the air-fryer and air-fry for 20 minutes without opening the drawer. Remove the Yorkshire puddings from the ramekins and serve immediately.

# WHOLE SWEET POTATOES

**4 medium sweet potatoes**
**1 tablespoon olive oil**
**1 teaspoon salt**
**toppings of your choice**

**SERVES 4 AS A SIDE OR SNACK**

The soft flesh of roasted sweet potatoes is delicious served with a savoury filling as a light meal or simply with some butter or oil and salt as a side dish.

Preheat the air-fryer to 200°C/400°F.

Wash and remove any imperfections from the skin of the sweet potatoes, then rub the potatoes with the olive oil and salt.

Add the sweet potatoes to the preheated air-fryer and air-fry for up to 40 minutes (the cooking time depends on the size of the potatoes). Remove as soon as they are soft when pierced. Slice open and serve with your choice of toppings.

### VARIATION: WHOLE JACKET POTATOES

Regular baking potatoes can be air-fried in the same way, but will require a cooking time of 45–60 minutes, depending on their size.

# SWEET THINGS

# BREAKFAST MUFFINS

1 eating apple, cored and grated

40 g/2 heaped tablespoons
   maple syrup

40 ml/3 tablespoons oil
   (avocado, olive or coconut),
   plus extra for greasing

1 egg

40 ml/3 tablespoons milk
   (plant-based if you wish)

90 g/scant ¾ cup brown rice flour

50 g/½ cup ground almonds

¾ teaspoon ground cinnamon

⅛ teaspoon ground cloves

¼ teaspoon salt

1 teaspoon baking powder

Greek or plant-based yogurt and
   fresh fruit, to serve

**MAKES 4**

Apple, cinnamon and cloves combine to create these deliciously filling and marvellously comforting breakfast muffins.

In a bowl mix the grated apple, maple syrup, oil, egg and milk. In another bowl mix the rice flour, ground almonds, cinnamon, cloves, salt and baking powder. Combine the wet ingredients with the dry, mixing until there are no visible patches of the flour mixture left. Grease 4 ramekins and divide the batter equally between them.

Preheat the air-fryer to 160°C/325°F.

Add the ramekins to the preheated air-fryer and air-fry for 12 minutes. Check the muffins are cooked by inserting a cocktail stick/toothpick into the middle of one of the muffins. If it comes out clean, the muffins are ready; if not, cook for a further couple of minutes.

Allow to cool in the ramekins, then remove and serve with your choice of yogurt and fresh fruit.

150 g/1 heaped cup rolled oats/
quick-cooking oats
50 g/⅓ cup dark chocolate chips
or buttons
300 ml/1¼ cups milk or plant-
based milk
50 g/3½ tablespoons Greek or
plant-based yogurt
1 tablespoon runny honey or
maple syrup
½ teaspoon ground cinnamon or
ground ginger
65 g/scant ⅓ cup smooth peanut
butter

**MAKES 9 SQUARES**

# PEANUT BUTTER &
# CHOCOLATE BAKED OATS

Deliciously moist nutty and chocolatey baked oats
are so quick and easy to make in the air-fryer.

Stir all the ingredients together in a bowl, then transfer to
a baking dish that fits your air-fryer drawer.

Preheat the air-fryer to 180°C/350°F.

Add the baking dish to the preheated air-fryer and air-fry
for 10 minutes. Remove from the air-fryer and serve hot, cut
into 9 squares.

100 g/7 tablespoons butter (or
plant-based spread if you wish)
75 g/5 tablespoons maple syrup
2 ripe bananas, mashed well with
the back of a fork
1 teaspoon vanilla extract
240 g/2½ cups rolled oats/
quick-cooking oats

**MAKES 9 SQUARES**

# BANANA MAPLE FLAPJACK

A simple five-ingredient flapjack that uses the natural
sugars and moistness of bananas to reduce the need for
added sugar.

Gently heat the butter and maple syrup in a medium saucepan
over a low heat until melted. Stir in the mashed banana, vanilla
and oats and combine all ingredients. Pour the flapjack mixture
into a 15 x 15-cm/6 x 6-in. baking pan and cover with foil.

Preheat the air-fryer to 200°C/400°F.

Add the baking pan to the preheated air-fryer and air-fry
for 12 minutes, then remove the foil and cook for a further
4 minutes to brown the top. Leave to cool before cutting into
9 squares.

# PECAN & MOLASSES FLAPJACK

**120 g/¹/₂ cup plus 2 teaspoons butter or plant-based spread, plus extra for greasing**

**40 g/2 tablespoons blackstrap molasses**

**60 g/5 tablespoons unrefined sugar**

**50 g/¹/₂ cup chopped pecans**

**200 g/1¹/₂ cups porridge oats/ steelcut oats (not rolled or jumbo)**

**MAKES 9 SQUARES**

The comfort of a sweet and nutty flapjack, but with the childhood memory of molasses makes for a real treat.

Preheat the air-fryer to 180°C/350°F.

Grease and line a 15 x 15-cm/6 x 6-in. baking pan.

In a large saucepan melt the butter/spread, molasses and sugar. Once melted, stir in the pecans, then the oats. As soon as they are combined, tip the mixture into the prepared baking pan and cover with foil.

Place the foil-covered baking pan in the preheated air-fryer and air-fry for 10 minutes. Remove the foil, then cook for a further 2 minutes to brown the top. Leave to cool, then cut into 9 squares.

# GRAIN-FREE MILLIONAIRE'S SHORTBREAD

## BASE

60 g/5 tablespoons coconut oil
1 tablespoon maple syrup
½ teaspoon vanilla extract
180 g/1¾ cups ground almonds
a pinch of salt

## MIDDLE

185 g/1⅓ cups dried pitted dates
    (soak in hot water for at least
    20 minutes, then drain)
2 tablespoons almond butter
90 g/scant ½ cup canned coconut
    milk (the thick part once it has
    separated is ideal)

## TOPPING

125 g/½ cup coconut oil
4 tablespoons cacao powder
1 tablespoon maple syrup

**MAKES 9 SQUARES**

This is a healthier grain-free take on a traditional millionaire's shortbread as it uses the air-fryer to create a crisp and golden base for the naturally sweetened caramel and chocolate toppings.

Preheat the air-fryer to 180°C/350°F.

To make the base, in a small saucepan melt the coconut oil with the maple syrup and vanilla extract. As soon as the coconut oil is melted, stir in the almonds and the salt off the heat. Press this mixture into a 15 x 15-cm/6 x 6-in. baking pan.

Add the baking pan to the preheated air-fryer and cook for 4 minutes, until golden brown on top. Remove from the air-fryer and allow to cool.

In a food processor, combine the rehydrated drained dates, almond butter and coconut milk. Once the base is cool, pour this mixture over the base and pop into the freezer to set for an hour.

After the base has had 45 minutes in the freezer, make the topping by heating the coconut oil in a saucepan until melted, then whisk in the cacao powder and maple syrup off the heat to make a chocolate syrup. Leave this to cool for 15 minutes, then pour over the set middle layer and return to the freezer for 30 minutes. Cut into 9 squares to serve.

# GRANOLA

60 g/¼ cup runny honey
50 g/3 tablespoons coconut oil
1 teaspoon vanilla extract
100 g/¾ cup jumbo rolled oats/
   old-fashioned oats (not
   porridge oats)
50 g/½ cup chopped walnuts
1 teaspoon ground cinnamon

**SERVES 3**

Made in under 10 minutes, this tasty granola is crunchy and perfect served with Greek yogurt and fresh fruit.

Preheat the air-fryer to 180°C/350°F.

Place the honey, coconut oil and vanilla extract in a small dish. Add this to the preheated air-fryer for 1 minute to melt.

In a small bowl combine the oats, nuts and cinnamon. Add the melted honey mixture and toss well, ensuring all the oats and nuts are well coated.

Lay an air-fryer liner or a pierced piece of parchment paper on the base of the air-fryer drawer. Add the granola mix on top, spread evenly in one layer. Air-fry for 4 minutes, then stir before cooking for a further 3 minutes. Leave to cool completely before serving or storing in a jar.

# OAT-COVERED BANANA FRITTERS

3 tablespoons plain/all-purpose
   flour (gluten-free if you wish)
1 egg, beaten
90 g/3 oz. oatcakes (gluten-free
   if you wish) or oat-based
   cookies, crushed to a crumb
   consistency
1½ teaspoons ground cinnamon
1 tablespoon unrefined sugar
4 bananas, peeled

**SERVES 4**

This is a much healthier take on a batter-coated and deep-fried banana fritter. It's no less delicious and even provides some wholegrain benefits.

Preheat the air-fryer to 180°C/350°F.

Set up three bowls – one with flour, one with beaten egg and the other with the oatcake crumb, cinnamon and sugar mixed together. Coat the bananas in flour, then in egg, then in the crumb mixture.

Add the bananas to the preheated air-fryer and air-fry for 10 minutes. Serve warm.

# CINNAMON-MAPLE PINEAPPLE KEBABS

4 x pineapple strips, roughly
    2 x 2 cm/³/₄ x ³/₄ in. by length
    of pineapple
1 teaspoon maple syrup
½ teaspoon vanilla extract
¼ teaspoon ground cinnamon
Greek or plant-based yogurt and
    grated lime zest, to serve

SERVES 2

Simple and effective, air-frying pineapple brings out
even greater sweetness and flavour.

Line the air-fryer with an air-fryer liner or a piece of pierced
parchment paper. Preheat the air-fryer to 180°C/350°F.

Stick small metal skewers through the pineapple lengthways.
Mix the maple syrup and vanilla extract together, then drizzle
over the pineapple and sprinkle over the cinnamon.

Add the skewers to the preheated lined air-fryer and air-fry
for 15 minutes, turning once. If there is any maple-vanilla
mixture left after the initial drizzle, then drizzle this over the
pineapple during cooking too. Serve with yogurt and lime zest.

# GRILLED GINGER & COCONUT PINEAPPLE RINGS

1 medium pineapple
coconut oil, melted
1½ teaspoons coconut sugar
½ teaspoon ground ginger
coconut or vanilla yogurt,
    to serve

SERVES 4

Perfect for a simple dessert when dining with friends.
Coconut, ginger and pineapple are a great match and
combine beautifully in this recipe.

Preheat the air-fryer to 180°C/350°F.

Peel and core the pineapple, then slice into 4 thick rings.

Mix together the melted coconut oil with the sugar and
ginger in a small bowl. Using a pastry brush, paint this mixture
all over the pineapple rings, including the sides of the rings.

Add the rings to the preheated air-fryer and air-fry for
20 minutes. Check after 18 minutes as pineapple sizes vary and
your rings may be perfectly cooked already. You'll know they are
ready when they're golden in colour and a fork can easily be
inserted with very little resistance

Serve warm with a generous spoonful of yogurt.

# BAKED NECTARINES

2 teaspoons maple syrup
1 teaspoon vanilla extract
1 teaspoon ground cinnamon
4 nectarines, halved and stones/
   pits removed
chopped nuts, yogurt and runny
   honey, to serve (optional)

**SERVES 4**

Air-frying nectarines brings out their natural sweetness and the addition of maple syrup, vanilla and cinnamon mellows the taste even further.

Preheat the air-fryer to 180°C/350° F.

Mix the maple syrup, vanilla extract and cinnamon in a ramekin or shake in a jar to combine. Lay the nectarine halves on an air-fryer liner or piece of pierced parchment paper. Drizzle over the maple syrup mix.

Place in the preheated air-fryer and air-fry for 9–11 minutes, until soft when pricked with a fork. Serve scattered with chopped nuts and with a generous dollop of yogurt. Drizzle over some honey if you wish.

# APPLE CRUMBLE

2 apples (each roughly 175 g/
   6 oz.), cored and chopped into
   2-cm/³/₄-in cubes
3 tablespoons unrefined sugar
100 g/1 cup jumbo rolled oats/
   old-fashioned oats
40 g/heaped ¼ cup flour
   (gluten-free if you wish)
1 heaped teaspoon ground
   cinnamon
70 g/scant ⅓ cup cold butter,
   chopped into small cubes

**SERVES 4**

A firm family favourite dessert for many, easily created using the air-fryer. Serve with a little plain yogurt or some custard/crème anglaise.

Preheat the air-fryer to 180°C/350°F.

Scatter the apple pieces in a baking dish that fits your air-fryer, then sprinkle over 1 tablespoon sugar. Add the baking dish to the preheated air-fryer and air-fry for 5 minutes.

Meanwhile, in a bowl mix together the oats, flour, remaining sugar and cold butter. Use your fingertips to bring the crumble topping together.

Remove the baking dish from the air-fryer and spoon the crumble topping over the partially cooked apple. Return the baking dish to the air dryer and air-fry for a further 10 minutes. Serve warm or cold.

# INDEX

## A

air-frying 7–8
all-day breakfast 42
almond butter: lime-almond satay sauce 87
almonds: grain-free chicken katsu 64
    grain-free millionaire's shortbread 135
    maple trail mix 17
apples: apple crumble 140
    breakfast muffins 128
    katsu sauce 64
apricot lamb burgers 47
arancini 102
asparagus spears 116
    sea bass with asparagus spears 79
aubergines/eggplant:
    aubergine parmigiana 94
    baba ganoush 35
    baked aubergine slices with yogurt dressing 109
avocado fries 27

## B

baba ganoush 35
bacon: all-day breakfast 42
    crispy bacon 13
bananas: banana maple flapjack 131
    oat-covered banana fritters 136
basil: pesto salmon 80
beef: beef adana kebabs 51
    Mediterranean beef meatballs 52
    simple steaks 56
    teriyaki steak skewers 56
bell peppers see peppers
bocconcini balls 32
bread: French toast 13
    miso mushrooms on sourdough toast 106
    pitta pizza 39
    sourdough croutons 9
    toast 10
breadcrumbs 9
    arancini 102
    beef adana kebabs 51
    chicken Kiev 72
    chicken Milanese 71
    Mediterranean beef meatballs 52
    muhammara 35
    oat & Parmesan crusted fish fillets 84
    Parmesan-coated fish fingers 84

pizza chicken nuggets 62
pork schnitzel 55
breakfast, all-day 42
breakfast muffins 128
broccoli, crispy 112
Brussels sprouts, roasted 115
burgers: apricot lamb burgers 47
    mini Moroccan lamb burgers 47
    Thai turkey burgers 68
butter, garlic 72
butternut squash 116
    butternut squash falafel 105

## C

Cajun fish fingers 83
Cajun prawn skewers 83
caper dressing 79
caramelised walnuts & pecans 17
carrots: cumin shoestring carrots 28
    katsu sauce 64
    spring rolls 31
cauliflower, crispy sweet & spicy 112
cheese: aubergine parmigiana 94
    baked feta, tomato & garlic pasta 98
    bocconcini balls 32
    cheese scones 36
    cheese, tomato & pesto crustless quiches 97
    chicken Milanese 71
    courgette fries 27
    crispy broccoli 112
    flat mushroom pizzas 93
    goat's cheese tartlets 97
    halloumi croutons 14
    halloumi fries 32
    oat & Parmesan crusted fish fillets 84
    Parmesan-coated fish fingers 84
    pesto salmon 80
    pitta pizza 39
    pizza chicken nuggets 62
    quinoa-stuffed romano peppers 90
    saganaki 98
    two-step pizza 93
chicken: chicken fajitas 60
    chicken Kiev 72
    chicken Milanese 71
    chicken tikka 67
    cornflake chicken nuggets 63

grain-free chicken katsu 64
    Korean chicken wings 68
    pizza chicken nuggets 62
    satay chicken skewers 67
    simple chicken nuggets 63
    spring rolls 31
    sticky chicken tikka drumsticks 71
    whole chicken 72
chickpeas: butternut squash patties 105
    chickpea falafel 105
    crispy chickpeas 14
chips see fries
chocolate: grain-free millionaire's shortbread 135
    peanut butter & chocolate baked oats 131
cilantro see coriander
cinnamon-maple pineapple kebabs 139
coconut: maple trail mix 17
coconut milk: satay chicken skewers 67
    satay tofu skewers 90
cod: cod in Parma ham 76
    crispy Cajun fish fingers 83
    Parmesan-coated fish fingers 84
coriander/cilantro:
    chickpea falafel 105
    mini Moroccan lamb burgers 47
    spring rolls 31
corn kernels see sweetcorn
cornflake chicken nuggets 63
cornmeal see polenta
courgettes/zucchini:
    chicken fajitas 60
    courgette fries 27
    katsu sauce 64
    Mediterranean vegetables 119
    Thai turkey burgers 68
croutons: halloumi croutons 14
    sourdough croutons 9
crumble, apple 140
cucumber: tzatziki 51
cumin shoestring carrots 28
curry: chicken tikka 67
    grain-free chicken katsu 64
    satay chicken skewers 67
    satay tofu skewers 90

## D E

dates: grain-free millionaire's shortbread 135
dips: baba ganoush 35
    muhammara 35
    tzatziki 51
dressings: caper dressing 79
    yogurt dressing 109
eggplants see aubergines
eggs: all-day breakfast 42
    cheese, tomato & pesto crustless quiches 97
    French toast 13
    Scotch eggs 36
    shakshuka 101
    soft-boiled/cooked eggs 10
equipment 8

## F

fajitas, chicken 60
falafel: butternut squash 105
    chickpea 105
fish: crispy Cajun fish fingers 83
    fish in foil 79
    oat & Parmesan crusted fish fillets 84
    see also cod, sea bass etc
fishcakes: store-cupboard fishcakes 80
    Thai-style tuna fishcakes 87
flapjack: banana maple flapjack 131
    pecan & molasses flapjack 132
French toast 13
fries: avocado fries 27
    courgette fries 27
    halloumi fries 32
    plantain fries 23
    polenta fries 24
    potato fries 20
    swede fries 23
    sweet potato fries 20
    wholegrain pitta chips 39
fritters, oat-covered banana 136

## G H

garlic: baba ganoush 35
    garlic & pepper pork chops 48
    garlic butter 72
    garlic-parsley prawns 87
ginger: grilled ginger & coconut pineapple rings 139

goat's cheese tartlets 97
golden raisins *see* sultanas
grain-free chicken katsu 64
grain-free millionaire's shortbread 135
granola 136
halloumi croutons 14
halloumi fries 32
ham: cod in Parma ham 76
hasselback new potatoes 123
honey: granola 136
  honey & mustard sausages with potatoes, peppers & onions 44
  honey roast parsnips 115

**K L**
katsu sauce 64
kebabs *see* skewers
king prawns/jumbo shrimp:
  Cajun prawn skewers 83
  garlic-parsley prawns 87
koftas, lamb 52
Korean chicken wings 68
lamb: apricot lamb burgers 47
  herby lamb chops 48
  lamb koftas 52
  mini Moroccan lamb burgers 47
lardons, crispy 13
lime-almond satay sauce 87

**M**
maple syrup: banana maple flapjack 131
  cinnamon-maple pineapple kebabs 139
  maple trail mix 17
Mediterranean beef meatballs 52
Mediterranean sauce 102
Mediterranean vegetables 119
millionaire's shortbread, grain-free 135
mini Moroccan lamb burgers 47
mini peppers *see* peppers
miso mushrooms on sourdough toast 106
muffins, breakfast 128
muhammara 35
mushrooms: all-day breakfast 42
  flat mushroom pizzas 93
  miso mushrooms on sourdough toast 106

**N O**
nectarines, baked 140
oats: apple crumble 140
  banana maple flapjack 131
  granola 136
  oat & Parmesan crusted fish fillets 84
  oat-covered banana fritters 136
  peanut butter & chocolate baked oats 131
  pecan & molasses flapjack 132
olives: patatas bravas 120
onions: beef adana kebabs 51
  honey & mustard sausages with potatoes, peppers & onions 44
  Mediterranean vegetables 119
  shakshuka 101

**P**
Parma ham, cod in 76
Parmesan-coated fish fingers 84
parsley: garlic-parsley prawns 87
parsnips, honey roast 115
pasta: baked feta, tomato & garlic pasta 98
patatas bravas 120
patties, butternut squash 105
peanut butter: peanut butter & chocolate baked oats 131
  satay chicken skewers 67
pecans: caramelised walnuts & pecans 17
  maple trail mix 17
  pecan & molasses flapjack 132
peppers (bell): beef adana kebabs 51
  chicken fajitas 60
  goat's cheese tartlets 97
  honey & mustard sausages with potatoes, peppers & onions 44
  Mediterranean sauce 102
  Mediterranean vegetables 119
  muhammara 35
  quinoa-stuffed romano peppers 90
  shakshuka 101
  spring rolls 31
  sweet & spicy mini peppers 120
  whole mini peppers 28
pesto: cheese, tomato & pesto crustless quiches 97
  goat's cheese tartlets 97
  pesto salmon 80
pine nuts: pesto salmon 80
pineapple: cinnamon-maple pineapple kebabs 139
  grilled ginger & coconut pineapple rings 139
pitta breads: pitta pizza 39
  wholegrain pitta chips 39
pizzas: flat mushroom pizzas 93
  pitta pizza 39
  pizza chicken nuggets 62
  two-step pizza 93
plantain fries 23
polenta fries 24
pork: garlic & pepper pork chops 48
  pork schnitzel 55
potatoes: hasselback new potatoes 123
  honey & mustard sausages with potatoes, peppers & onions 44
  patatas bravas 120
  potato fries 20
  store-cupboard fishcakes 80
  Thai-style tuna fishcakes 87
  whole jacket potatoes 124
prawns/shrimp: Cajun prawn skewers 83
  garlic-parsley prawns 87

**Q R**
quiches: cheese, tomato & pesto crustless quiches 97
quinoa-stuffed romano peppers 90
rice: arancini 102
rice paper wrappers: spring rolls 31
rutabaga *see* swede

**S**
saganaki 98
salmon, pesto 80
satay chicken skewers 67
satay sauce, lime-almond 87
satay tofu skewers 90
sauces: katsu sauce 64
  lime-almond satay sauce 87
  Mediterranean sauce 102
  pizza sauce 93
sausagemeat: Scotch eggs 36
sausages: honey & mustard sausages with potatoes, peppers & onions 44
scones, cheese 36
Scotch eggs 36
sea bass with asparagus spears 79
shakshuka 101
shortbread, grain-free millionaire's 135
shrimp *see* prawns
simple chicken nuggets 63
simple steaks 56
skewers: beef adana kebabs 51
  Cajun prawn skewers 83
  chicken tikka 67
  cinnamon-maple pineapple kebabs 139
  lamb koftas 52
  satay chicken skewers 67
  satay tofu skewers 90
  teriyaki steak skewers 56
soft boiled eggs 10
sourdough croutons 9
soy sauce: Korean chicken wings 68
  teriyaki steak skewers 56
spring rolls 31
steak: simple steaks 56
  teriyaki steak skewers 56
sticky chicken tikka drumsticks 71
store-cupboard fishcakes 80
sultanas/golden raisins: maple trail mix 17
swede/rutabaga fries 23
sweet & spicy mini peppers 120
sweet potatoes: sweet potato fries 20
  whole sweet potatoes 124
sweetcorn/corn kernels: quinoa-stuffed romano peppers 90
  Thai-style tuna fishcakes 87

**T**
tahini: baba ganoush 35
  yogurt dressing 109
tartlets, goat's cheese 97
temperatures 8
teriyaki steak skewers 56
Thai turkey burgers 68
Thai-style tuna fishcakes 87

toast 10
  French toast 13
  miso mushrooms on
    sourdough toast 106
tofu: satay tofu skewers
  90
tomatoes: all-day
  breakfast 42
  aubergine parmigiana 94
  baked feta, tomato &
    garlic pasta 98

cheese, tomato & pesto
  crustless quiches 97
cod in Parma ham 76
flat mushroom pizzas 93
Mediterranean sauce 102
Mediterranean
  vegetables 119
patatas bravas 120
pitta pizza 39
pizza chicken nuggets 62
shakshuka 101
two-step pizza 93

trail mix, maple 17
tuna fishcakes, Thai-style
  87
turkey burgers, Thai 68
two-step pizza 93
tzatziki 51

**W Y Z**
walnuts: caramelised
  walnuts & pecans 17
  granola 136
  muhammara 35

whole chicken 72
whole jacket potatoes 124
whole mini peppers 28
whole sweet potatoes 124
wholegrain pitta chips 39
yogurt: chicken tikka 67
  sticky chicken tikka
    drumsticks 71
  tzatziki 51
  yogurt dressing 109
Yorkshire puddings 123
zucchini *see* courgettes

# ACKNOWLEDGEMENTS

I would like to thank my publishers Ryland, Peters & Small for approaching me with the concept of creating an air-fryer recipe book. Having seen just how popular air-fryers have become and using the number of recipes and videos across social media platforms as a measure of popularity, I am reminded once more that Ryland, Peters & Small have their fingers very much on the pulse. Julia Charles has once again provided excellent editorial direction and Cindy Richards, Leslie Harrington and Gillian Haslam have all played a key role in making this book a wonderful representation of simple and accessible air-fryer recipes. Claire Winfield has worked her magic by capturing beautiful photographs to accompany these carefully crafted recipes.

Jane Graham-Maw, my incredibly supportive literary agent, continues to work hard to create the best representation of my ability as a recipe creator. To my recipe testers Wendy Burdon, Louise Hale, Jo Bristow and Jodie Humphries, I would like to say a huge thank you. Your feedback has been wonderfully helpful.

This, my fourth book, created during the latter stages of a global pandemic, has been both a blessing and a frustration for my family who have been barred from the kitchen at times. Tempers have been frayed, but the rewards have been delicious and well worth it according to my teenagers. They have come to love the air-fryer too and, when the time comes, will be packed with one when they leave home for the first time, armed with this recipe book of course!

**JENNY TSCHIESCHE**
BSC (HONS), DIP (ION), FDSC BANT